Seduced by Japan:

A Memoir of the Days Spent with Angela Carter

with "Her Side of the Story" written by Natsumi Ikoma

Written by Sozo Araki

Translated, Annotated, and Introduced by Natsumi Ikoma

Contents

Introduction by the Translator	iii
Chapter 1	3
Chapter 2	25
Chapter 3	47
Chapter 4	68
Chapter 5	91
Chapter 6	115
Chapter 7	130
Epilogue: Angela Carter, Myself, and My Monster	146
Her Side of the Story (Afterword by the Translator)	153
Works Consulted	175

Introduction by the Translator

Natsumi Ikoma

Angela Carter was born Angela Olive Stalker in 1940 in Eastbourne, UK, and died of cancer in 1992, at the age of fifty-one. During her lifetime, she produced an abundance of works as a writer of fiction, a playwright, and a journalist. Critical acclaim for her works has steadily increased since her untimely death, with more postgraduate theses written on her work every year.

Though her life and her work have been the object of extensive scholarship, little is known about the years she spent in Japan. She arrived in Japan in 1969 with money from the Somerset Maugham Literary Award and lived in the Tokyo metropolis for a period of time before returning to England in 1972. During her sojourn, she produced not only *The Internal Desire Machines of Doctor Hoffman* (1972), but also many short stories and journalistic pieces on Japan, some of which touch upon the relationship she had with a Japanese man. That has been the extent to which her life in Japan was known; a hidden life considered 'mysterious'[1] until the recent publication of Carter's official biography, written by Edmund Gordon.[2]

---

[1] Gamble, Sarah, *Angela Carter: A Literary Life*. Palgrave Macmillan, 2006, p.106.
[2] Gordon, Edmund, *The Invention of Angela Carter: A Biography*. Chatto & Windus, 2016.

This memoir sheds light upon the penumbra of this 'mystery' partly revealed by the biography. The author of this memoir is the very person Angela Carter had a romantic relationship with between 1969 and 1971. She came back to Japan for him, after her brief first visit in 1969. Their romance was passionate and bittersweet, and the break-up, in the end, was painful for both.

The author of this memoir, Sozo Araki, whom Angela refers to as 'my friend S' in her essay on Mishima, was born in 1945 in Tokyo, the seventh son of a large family. His father was a graduate of the University of Tokyo and worked as a consultant for various organizations. His parents divorced when Sozo was a child. His surroundings were more open and international than conventional Japanese families; the eldest brother married an English woman, and an elder sister married a Jewish-Dutch man, at whose house Sozo stayed for a week – and learned to speak English – when he was seventeen years old. While at Waseda University, Sozo worked at a U.S. military base in Tachikawa, which helped him improve his English. Nourishing his dream to become a writer, Sozo quit university before graduation and was doing odd jobs, such as private tutoring and interpreting, when he met Angela.

It was late September 1969 in Tokyo when Sozo and Angela met. Sozo was a young man with an ambition to be a writer, and Angela – older by five years – was an established author with a literary award in hand. They were an instant match and began a relationship. Apparently, Angela Carter had not planned to stay long on this initial trip, and after several

Introduction by the Translator v

rendezvous, she returned to England, vowing to Sozo that she would soon return. She came back some months later, after having separated from her first husband in England. Angela and Sozo lived together in a residential area of Tokyo, and then moved to Kujukuri Beach in the neighbouring prefecture of Chiba. Their blissful life in this small seaside village is beautifully described in the memoir. Their romantic relationship, however, began to encounter difficulties. International relationships are rarely straightforward, especially forty-five years ago, when Japan was less globalised than today. It would, however, be simplistic to attribute the problems to mere cultural difference. The situation surrounding their separation was more complex and subtle. The ending scarred both, but Angela seems to have taken it more bitterly. This perhaps explains why she withheld details of her relationship with Sozo from the public. Her journals, archived now in the British Library, contain multiple entries about Sozo, some of which I include in the final section of this book in order to provide a complementing – and sometimes contradictory – narrative by Carter herself. The painful break-up did not prevent them from remaining friends – for a while. The communication tailed off after a few years. After Sozo, Angela had a brief relationship with a new boyfriend, a Korean man living in Japan, but the new relationship sputtered. In 1972, she left Japan permanently for England.

Two or three years after his separation from Angela Carter, Sozo married a Japanese woman. Having worked in various capacities, as an English teacher, translator, interpreter, and essay writer, he decided to go abroad to learn more about people, and found himself in Vancouver with his wife. He stayed a year, and upon returning to Japan, founded an English language school, nurturing it into a successful business. His interest waned and shifted to the field of counselling – likely prompted by a program he was involved with to cure stuttering, a speech disorder that afflicted both Sozo and Angela. As stated in this memoir, stuttering was Sozo's inner demon. In fact, during the interview with me, Sozo revealed that this demon was the real reason behind the break-up with Angela. He felt that unless he tackled his speech problem, he could never make it in any field. In this way, he was driven to explore stuttering and its meaning, the circle of interest widening until he came to terms with his own affliction. Sozo is now a man palpably at ease with himself. If he had been in his present state of mind, he adds ruefully, he would not have split with Angela. Sozo lives in Tokyo with his wife and is now a successful counsellor/writer with publications on human psychology, notably stalking, personal relationships, inferiority complexes – and, of course, stuttering.

From this intriguing memoir, I hope that readers will sense the importance of Angela's relationship with Sozo and the profound influence it had on her literary works and feminism. What if Angela had not met Sozo? What if she had not gone through this relationship? Tantalizingly, we are forced to ask whether the brilliant novels of later years would have emerged. We can detect the Japanese, particularly Sozo's influence, upon her works after reading this memoir. Angela

Introduction by the Translator vii

Carter was desperately in love with Sozo, and their romance, though rife with contradictions, difficulty, and pain, had a significant impact on Angela Carter as a writer.

It was by simple luck and coincidence that I met Sozo Araki. One day, an email came from a person who found me on the Internet as an academic scholar specializing in the works of Angela Carter. She wrote to me, saying she knew a man who claimed to be an ex-boyfriend of Angela Carter: 'Do you want to meet him?' I was sceptical. Who wouldn't be? We met in a coffee shop in downtown Shinjuku, where Sozo and Angela first met almost forty years prior. Sozo was sitting in a chair, a man probably in his sixties, with black hair and piercing eyes. He wore a Mackintosh coat over a suit. Undoubtedly, a handsome man then and now. He was not a businessman, but rather, he had the manner of a writer, college lecturer, or doctor, who moved about his world with freedom and authority. The moment we started our conversation, I knew. This is the real thing: the Japanese ex-boyfriend of Angela Carter. The minor details he gave on their relationship fit precisely with what Angela wrote in her pieces on Japan, details barely known to Japanese readers outside the realm of academia. It was obvious that Sozo was not a Carter scholar, nor even an avid reader of her novels. Still, he knew so much about this woman during her stay in Japan.

After this first meeting, we met several times to talk about Angela Carter. Initially, the reason was plain curiosity: both academic and personal. I am a huge admirer of her work. Besides, her life in Japan was unknown territory. Sozo's stories were fascinating, full of anecdotes and various episodes, some of which were later fictionalized and narrated by Carter herself. Sozo has a certain charm, and I could see why Angela Carter fell in love with him. Once, I was Angela. We strolled in the park together, Sozo snd I.

Later, in the British Library archive studying Carter's journals, I found numerous entries referring to Sozo. She describes him as 'incredibly beautiful' (Gordon 140), expressing the admiration Carter had for Sozo's beauty. He was an object. She appreciated it; she walked around him like an art connoisseur. In the same journal, later, she reveals the emotional turmoil that churned through their relationship. They quarrelled and she came to a conclusion that was not merely heart-wrenching, but devastating – she loved him more than anything but their relationship was doomed, and she had to leave him sooner or later.

I was convinced that Sozo's memories must be shared. He must write a memoir. He must return his memories to Angela Carter's world, to readers and scholars. Its interpretive impact would be evident. After some hesitation, he agreed. And here we are.

Angela Carter, in this memoir, is Angela through the prism of Sozo Araki. The reflection that shimmers here may diverge from that shown by Angela herself or her family. Certainly, the Angela in this memoir is a reconstruction: a piece of sculpture made from memory, with many alterations, angles, and misconceptions that memories are bound to contain. Yet, we find here an unmistakable trace of Angela Carter, the writer we know. The Angela in this memoir is a complex and contradictory being: beautiful, young, reckless, intelligent, timid, bold, romantic, and helplessly in love.

The romance between Angela and Sozo is described from beginning to end, with its joy, happiness, pain, shame, and remorse. In fact, it is an ordinary romance; it is a moment in the passage of youth. Its unique quality lies in the fact that it is an interracial relationship, and also because of the time period. From this memoir, the reader can learn much about the social situation of Tokyo, in 1969 and 1971. It teases and reveals much about Japanese customs, ways of life, and Japanese views on foreigners, especially Caucasians. With such things teeming in the background of her affair, Angela Carter became 'radicalized' as a feminist and a writer of fiction. My modest hope is that this memoir, published in English, together with "Her Side of the Story" written by myself as an afterword, will bring forth an additional understanding, an augmented appreciation of Angela Carter's works and perhaps new insights to the ever-growing body of critical scholarship. This memoir intends to provoke new interest and a shift of focus from what may sometimes be viewed as an adventitious and mildly interesting episode in 'another place' to something that is indeed a central and critical event yet to be explored – the Japanese connection.

Part of this book project was supported by JSPS KAKENHI Grant Number JP24520307, which I truly appreciate. I also would like to write a few words of appreciation. First to Sozo

Araki, for agreeing to pen this memoir. How hard it is to confess in a memoir, to be reminded of and make public, a private pain. I would also like to thank Prof Patricia Waugh of Durham University, who supervised my Ph.D. research and first recommended Angela Carter to me. I would like also to recognise the help given by Prof John Maher and Prof Christoper Simons for reading the manuscript and polishing it up. I am immensely indebted to Dr Lindsay Ray Morrison who was a very talented Ph.D. student at the Graduate School of International Christian University at the time of my writing for providing me with valuable assistance and for painstakingly proof-reading. I am also indebted to Mr Koichi Shimomura, editor at Eihosha publishing company, for his assistance and patience. Many other friends, family, colleagues, and students offered emotional support and inspiration for which I am very thankful. Without them, this project could have never been realised. Last but not least, I would like to thank Angela Carter herself, for her wonderful works and the inspiration she has given me. I wish you were still alive, so that I could speak with you today. I started my Ph.D. in 1998, much too late. You were already gone. However, this memoir was a personal encounter. I could reach out to you, meet, hear, and feel your younger self. For this, I am eternally grateful.

July 2017
Natsumi Ikoma
Professor of British and Japanese Literature,
International Christian University, Tokyo, Japan

Seduced by Japan:

A Memoir of the Days Spent with Angela Carter

with "Her Side of the Story" written by Natsumi Ikoma

Chapter 1

The First Encounter

It was one day in early autumn, 1969, late September or early October. A refreshing sunny afternoon after a very hot summer. I went to Shinjuku on the Keio Line and went through the main exit of Shinjuku station. My usual route. Dodging the crowd with my long strides, I walked along Main Street. Four or five minutes later, I was pushing through the throng of young men and women and standing in front of a big café called Fugetsudo.[1] I peeked through the massive window. Packed, as usual.

As usual, I scanned the ground floor then took the stairs up. The room upstairs was smaller. At a glance, I knew the woman I came to see was not there, nor did any other woman grab my attention.

I returned to the ground floor, drifting to the farthest end of the café. I spied a foreign woman sitting by the window, looking in my direction. The moment I saw her, the brief conversation we had at Fugetsudo the previous day came flooding

---

[1] Fugetsudo: a famous café located in Shinjuku. It started as a café that played classical music and thrived from 1946-1973, attracting many young artists and foreigners.

back. We'd been sitting in a seat near to the entrance, if I remember correctly. I'd started up a conversation with the foreign woman: 'Hello, where are you from?' 'From England,' she replied. 'Sightseeing? Business?' I asked. She was all smiles, for reasons that escaped me. 'Sightseeing,' she said. That conversation flashed back to my mind vividly. At the time, I had been waiting for a young Japanese woman, who appeared shortly after. On that day, therefore, my conversation with the foreign woman was cut short.

When I realized that it was the same foreign woman eyeing me, I put on a nonchalant smile and called out, 'Hi,' or something like that to her. Seeing the seat next to hers was unoccupied, I asked, 'Mind if I sit here?' She smiled back, saying, 'Not at all.' I sat with my shoulders brushing hers. She looked at me and cracked a smile again.

She was wearing a thin jacket, between red and pink, with the sleeves rolled up. Perhaps she was wearing jeans. Her face and arms, sticking out of the jacket, were red with sunburn. She followed my gaze and said, 'I went to the beach in Hawaii.'

I could not guess her age. If she had said twenty-eight, I would have taken it as true. If she had said thirty-eight, I would have believed it. Her age was really not a matter of concern to me. What I remember is that, sitting next to her, I felt good, at ease, with no strangeness or nervous tension. Caucasians typically exude a lascivious aura, that which carnivorous animals emit. It is attractive, but often intimidating and too rich for Northern Asian senses. As I took a seat next to her, however, I did not at all feel an oppressive aura characteristic of Caucasians. I felt relaxed sitting next to her from the start.

I do not recall what we talked about after that. The only thing I remember is that part of the conversation somehow led to the topic of youth riots, taking place all over the world in those days. I said, 'It's fine that young people in Tokyo, or California, or the Latin Quarter of Paris demonstrate or go on strike, but they are not really fighting for a more ideal, more liberal, or even better society. In the end, these riots are just commonplace generational conflict: the young rebelling against the old. What is ironic, pathetic about those conflicts is this: the young soon grow old. Before they know it, they are all old. They find they've worked their asses off to pay off the mortgage and educate their children. Their wars will soon be a good old memory of student days, just like a school club. Ha ha ha ha.'

To my somewhat ridiculing tone, she reproached me with a grave expression on her face, 'To most people, surely, it may become a memory like a school activity, but to others, the experience may come to have deeper significance.' I was struck by her seriousness. At the same time, I noticed she tended to stutter when she spoke.

We went on talking for a long time. After an hour or two, I asked her, 'You're not hungry? Why don't we grab something to eat?' 'I've been waiting for you to say that,' she replied with a smile on her face. 'Let's get out of here, then.'

In my mind, I told myself, 'This woman knows how to lead

a man on. Or perhaps, she simply doesn't hesitate when expressing her real feelings…' I also felt, 'If she really felt so, as she said, she should have taken the initiative herself.' Regardless, I got on my feet and urged her to go.

Entrance of Fugetsudo[2]

The Ground Floor of Fugetsudo

---

[2] Photographs taken by Akio Kawasumi. Reproduced by courtesy of Kawasumi Kobayashi Kenji Photograph Office.

Chapter 1

View from the First Floor[3]

When we stepped outside, the sun was already setting. It was a very pleasant, early autumn dusk. We went along Shinjuku Street and leisurely walked by Isetan department store[4] toward the direction of Yasukuni Street. The woman was a couple of inches taller than I was (and I was only a little bit taller than the average Japanese male in those days), but I did not feel uncomfortable walking side by side. Our conversation flowed.

It is strange. Whenever you walk side by side with someone with whom you have the right chemistry, man or woman, you feel relaxed from the start. Your stride naturally matches theirs. You don't have to keep up with the pace of the other; conversation flows effortlessly, never stumbles. On the other hand, when you are ill-matched, the strides do not jive, you

---

[3] Photograph reproduced by courtesy of Masuzawa Architect & Associates.
[4] Isetan: a well-known department store in Shinjuku.

both strain to adjust to the other person's pace. Your conversation leads to awkward silences, whether the topic is interesting or not. In our case, the woman and myself, the chemistry was just right. For sure.

I spotted a reasonable-looking *sushi* restaurant a short distance from Yasukuni Street. We bobbed under the curtain at the entrance. I was simpleminded, I thought *sushi* was a good idea for a foreign woman. We sat at the counter and ordered an inexpensive set of *sushi* for two with beer.

The woman did not seem to marvel at the sight of *sushi* arranged neatly before her. She started eating the *sashimi* nonchalantly, as if she was a regular.

'You've eaten raw fish before?' I asked.

'Not like in *sushi*. It's my first time,' she replied.

'How is it? Good?'

'Yes, good,' she said, again with a nonchalant tone.

In those days, around 1970, this was not the usual reaction from Americans or English I took to *sushi* restaurants. As soon as they learned it was raw fish, they either grimaced, 'No way!' and wouldn't touch it, or they would cautiously try it. When they realized it was delicious, they would exaggeratedly say, 'Oh. It is very, *very* good!'

By the time we left the *sushi* place, it was completely dark. I do not remember what route we took. I led her back to the Shinjuku station area. I took her to one of those big bars for young people. They were called '*kompa*' in those days.

On an enormous floor were several round-shaped bars and in the middle of each, a young bartender quietly working. All the customers turned around and stared. I was with a white woman. We sat at the bar at the centre. I ordered a martini. The woman thought for a moment and ordered a weak Bloody Mary.

She surveyed the customers around us with curiosity and asked me in a low voice, 'Are those women hostesses?' It seemed she was more interested in the pleasure quarter's subculture than in *sushi*.

'They're customers. This kind of place doesn't offer a hostess service,' I answered and added, 'The bars with hostess service are too expensive for me.'

For some reason, she smiled in delight. When the smile faded, a nervous and helpless look crept across her face. The shoulders that had seemed wide a moment ago now appeared thin and narrow. She looked at me as if in need of help. It dawned on me that the woman wanted me to kiss her. So, though uneasy about the other customers spying on us, I drew my face closer to hers and kissed her on the lips. She responded passionately.

I thought I needed to come up with something seductive to say. 'What should I say on an occasion like this?' I quickly racked my brain, but nothing dishy came out… I needed to say something, however… So, I whispered in her ear, 'Where shall we go?' I cursed myself, 'What a stupid thing to say!' But, to my pathetic question, the woman gave a wonderful reply. Drawing close to my ear, she whispered, 'This is your town.' Secretly excited, I grasped her hand and mumbled, 'Yeah, you're right.'

Too embarrassed to leave the bar straightaway after this exchange, I took my time and drank up the martini very slowly. After I finished, I took the woman's hand again and left the bar. When we were outside, Shinjuku at night-time was filled with lively crowds, as always. Each person in the crowd was strolling along, anticipating something spectacular.

I took the woman to the station's south exit and continued towards Yoyogi. Beyond the busiest quarter, lit by gaudy neon signs, was a border-town area where a handful of shabby wooden inns stood in a cluster. At the time, they were called '*tsurekomi*'[5]: inns used by men and women for sex.

I opened the entrance door of the first place. I think I recall that the door was not Western-style but a sliding door, in the traditional Japanese style.

'*Irasshaai.*'[6]

With that cheery greeting, a middle-aged maid came out from the back. Her smile froze the moment she saw her guest was with a white woman. She recovered and renewed her smile, 'Here for a rest? Or will you be staying the night?'

A 'rest' refers to renting a room for love-making for two hours. 'Short stay, short stay,' I joked, grinning and pretending to be casual.

Whenever I came to such a place, I could not help but pretend to be an experienced player. Unable to go in there with a business-like manner made me acutely aware of just how

---

[5] *Tsurekomi*: literally, a place to take someone into.

[6] *Irasshai*: this is a usual greeting phrase.

inexperienced I was.

'Right. Then come to the room upstairs,' she said. We removed our shoes and followed her up a narrow, creaking staircase to a room at the end of the corridor. The door was a thin *fusuma*,[7] and the room itself was only about four and a half *tatami*[8] mats. In the middle was one *futon*. That was it. A light bulb with a pink shade dangled from the ceiling.

The maid said, 'A short stay is 1,600 yen.'[9] Was it 1,200 yen? 1,400 yen? 1,600 yen? Below 2,000 yen for sure. Back then, I frequented these cheap inns. Whenever I managed to pick up a girl at Fugetsudo or some other café, a jazz *kissa*,[10] a bar, or on the street, I brought the girl to a *tsurekomi* like this one. *Tsurekomi* were favoured by men like me, who hunted for non-professional girls, though they were also used by cheap prostitutes and their customers.

A few days after that night, when I was bragging to a friend of mine about this 'adventure,' he said, 'What a cheek to take a respectable foreign woman who isn't a prostitute to such a shady inn. I would have at least selected a decent hotel, the best I could.' He stared at me, appalled.

---

[7] *Fusuma*: a sliding door made of paper with wooden frame.

[8] *Tatami*: *tatami* mats are a traditional kind of flooring in Japanese houses. Each *tatami* is a rectangular mat made of soft rush straw tightly woven with cloth edging. Because the size of a *tatami* is uniform, it is still used to measure the size of Japanese rooms, whether or not they have *tatami* flooring.

[9] Equivalent to US 15 dollars, in today's exchange rate.

[10] Jazz *kissa*: tea houses that play jazz usually from gramophone records. Customers mainly come to listen to the music. Popular in the 1920s in Japan, and revived in the 50s through the 60s.

At the time, however, it never occurred to me that my action constituted as 'taking a respectable foreign woman to a cheap, shady inn.' From my point of view, I just wanted privacy with this woman with the pale, white skin. I took her to a room that I could afford and was familiar with.

What did the English woman herself feel about being taken to such a shady hotel by a Japanese man whom she barely knew? On her second or third day in Japan? The one thing I know for sure is she did not find it repulsive.

The maid left and we were alone together. The woman abruptly drew her flushed face closer to mine, planting wet and passionate kisses on my face. After a while, she let go of me and undressed, unconcerned that the ceiling light was still on. Her face resembled a close-up from a Hollywood movie: Katharine Hepburn's bony face.

I knew the maid would be bringing tea any minute. I thought of stopping the woman, keeping things from going further. On second thought, it seemed rude to hold back when the woman was showing so much passion. So I took off my top, embraced the woman, and laid her down on the *futon*.

'I brought you some tea.'

The maid knocked on the *fusuma* and came right in, just as we were undressing. Instantly, the woman clung to me, burying her face in my chest, and shutting her eyes. We waited till she set down the tea and left. Familiar to such sights, she put down the tea and left noiselessly.

I gently peeled myself away from the woman and looked at her body again. I had never slept with a white woman. She had a solid bone structure, which seemed bigger than Japanese women's. Her skin was very white – whiter than I had expected; white as porcelain. She laid on her back, and gazed at me expectantly.

After our first embrace, we switched the light off and laid on the futon, talking in the darkness. Only then did we reveal our names. When I heard her name was 'Angela,' I remember saying, 'Nice name. Sounds Spanish,' and Angela replied, 'My mother was a romantic.'

I asked her age. Angela said 'twenty-nine.' I told her I was twenty-four, and she said, 'A good age.' I asked what she did for a living, to which she replied, 'I write novels.' Somehow, I took it to mean scribbling stories, hoping to publish them in a college journal or magazine of some literary circle. That's what everyone around me who declared themselves novelists did. Only that. So I thought she was one of them. Especially, when women say they're writing novels, the 'novels' always turn out to be badly-written stories in niche magazines.

She asked me what I did, so I said, 'I want to be a novelist, so now I'm studying various things for it. I tutor in English for a living.' Angela asked, 'Have you ever published?' I replied honestly, 'I've only published once in a student magazine.' I chose to classify this as a 'literary coterie' magazine.

'What kind of story did you write?' asked Angela.

'I once worked at an American military base when I was a student. I used the experience to write about the goings on between blacks and Japanese …'

'It sounds interesting. I'd really like to read it.'

'You need to learn Japanese, then.'

'It would take 10 years to read it… Are you interested in black people?'

'Yeah, the blacks in the U.S., because they were forced to live hellish lives for the sake of the whites, you see. I'm interested in the American Indians for the same reason.'

Angela was silent. She looked nervous, perhaps now that the topic had shifted to racial issues. I reckoned that talking seriously about blacks and the Native Americans was a kind of taboo for American whites. Maybe the British also found it difficult to deal with.

I returned to fiction.

'A friend of mine loves Dostoevsky, especially Alyosha. He wrote a story called, "Goodbye, My Alyosha."'

'I like that title.'

'Do you? Who do you like best in *The Brothers Karamazov*?'

'Grushenka. She's truly wonderful.'

I found Angela typical of a modern, intelligent woman. Her opinion was the kind of response a shallow feminist would give, I thought.

'Who do you like best?' Angela asked.

'The father,' I said.

This was not a display of originality. I really did find this man, so full of worldly desires, delightful somehow. He seemed, in fact, to be the only real human being in the novel. Angela guffawed in the darkness.

I look back now. There we were. Naked. Talking about

Dostoevsky, a few hours after we met. A revelation! Somewhere deep inside Angela's body and soul, conflicting elements lived, colliding noisily with each other. A naïve purity, a simplicity of mind, and her good nature existed side-by-side with an ice-cold intelligence. The foxy strength of a middle-aged woman and the fragility of a little girl appeared in alternate. Her shyness, which was so extreme as to make me pity her, coexisted with an unstoppable talkativeness and a definitive individuality. She possessed a naïve sense of justice and simultaneously a degree of immorality that was repulsive. I only started to notice these contradictions a year later.

The Morning After

The next morning, we went to Shinjuku again and parted ways for a while. Angela went back to the hotel she was staying in to get changed, take a shower, and do some things.

I killed time in the town. What did I do till I met up with Angela again? Most likely, I dropped in Kinokuniya bookshop[11] as usual, browsed the shelves. I might have played '*pachinko*.'[12] We arranged to meet again in front of Kinokuniya at 11am.

Angela showed up in an orange trouser-suit. Her hair was light brown with dark undertones, curled. She seemed to be wearing a spot of make-up. She smiled and said, 'Hi.' It gave off a showiness peculiar to white women, and completely

---

[11] Kinokuniya bookshop: a well-known, large bookshop in Shinjuku.

[12] *Pachinko*: a casino-like amusement facility with a particular type of game machine. Usually, people play them for money.

different from the subdued woman of the previous day. She also seemed happier than the day before. Like a Hollywood actress with a mind, I thought.

We walked through Shinjuku. I turned to her and said, 'I imagine Agatha Christie might have been like you.' Angela responded sullenly, 'Don't know anything about her. Never read her books.' I meant it as a compliment. To tell the truth, Agatha Christie was the only British woman author that came to mind. Angela is not pleased, I thought, 'She doesn't want to be in the same pack as popular writers like Agatha Christie. I guess she's in it for high literature.'

We entered a coffee shop and ordered two breakfasts: a cup of coffee, a piece of thick toast, and a boiled egg. I was garrulous, holding forth on the high literacy of the Japanese population. I noted that the literacy rate at the end of the Edo era was nearly fifty percent, much higher than the ten percent literacy rate of the French citizens when the French Revolution took place. I was eager to tell her how a large number of people in Japan read Euro-American writers, like Hemingway, Henry Miller, Alan Sillitoe, Sartre, and Camus. I wanted to impress her. I wanted to remind her that 'You're English but Japan really is an interesting country for an author like you.' Soon enough, Angela took the bait and responded excitedly, 'Japan really does seem attractive.' Angela asked, 'So, what Japanese works do you think I should read? Who do you recommend?' 'Jun'ichiro Tanizaki'[13] I said.

'Tanizaki? Which one?'

'They're all interesting. Just take one and read it.'

We left the coffee shop near the station, and walked on to Waseda, in the area of my old university. We strolled about. The university town was peppered with bookshops and cheap eating places. We walked around campus, and climbed a nearby hill. I took her there because I thought Angela would be interested in universities. She was an academic type. Simplemindedly, I thought she must have some interest in colleges, but she showed no interest whatsoever. Neither in the campus nor the town. 'Did you go to university?' I asked. Angela mentioned the name of a university. The name of a region I didn't know. 'University was boring,' she added.

In the afternoon, we had a meal and a coffee at a café (though they were not called 'cafés' in those days). Angela looked out of sorts. She seemed restless, nervous, and timid all at the same time. She reached out to hold my hand. Her hand was hot. 'Could you… perhaps?' When I asked, Angela's cheeks flushed and she nodded.

I took her to a *tsurekomi* near Takadanobaba station. Again, a look of surprise at seeing me with a white woman flickered for an instant across the face of the woman receptionist at the inn, but they led us upstairs without any fuss. In those days in the 1970s, many Japanese people did not know how to react to foreigners. No place actually banned them – restaurants, bars, or hotels. No places gave them bad service. It was just a lack

---

[13] Tanizaki Jun'ichiro (1886-1965): a major male author in modern Japanese literature whose work often reflects the identity crisis of Japanese culture in the face of Western influence in the Meiji to Taisho eras. His work also explores the sphere of sexuality and eroticism.

of familiarity with foreigners. There were not many in Japan at that time. I do not recall real prejudice against foreigners, nor anti-foreigner movements. The situation was the same for all of them, even African-Americans.

In the upstairs room of that inn, after passionate sex, Angela sat up cross-legged and brushed her hair and fixed her make-up. It was so unlike anything a Japanese woman would have done. There in front of me, with her purple-blue eyes and pale skin, I felt like I was watching a Hollywood movie.

Paperback

To tell the truth, the memory of that first encounter with Angela is vivid only up to this point. After that, until Angela briefly left Japan, there remain merely patches of recollection, in no particular chronological order. We had about ten days before she left Japan. We must have met up several times. Angela visited Kyoto and Nara so our dates could not have been numerous.

On one rendezvous, we were lying on the lawn of Shinjuku Gyoen, when Angela took out an English translation of Tanizaki's *The Makioka Sisters*. Her studiousness was impressive, but it was surprising to learn that the original title, *Sasame-yuki*, was translated to the tasteless *The Makioka Sisters*.

'What a boring English title,' I said. Angela asked me, 'What does the original title mean?' I pondered. How should I translate '*sasame-yuki?*' 'Fragile Snow,' I suggested. 'A wonderful translation,' Angela said.

I think it was the very same day, we were walking in the

underground shopping mall at Shinjuku west exit. Angela abruptly stopped in front of a bookshop and started checking the shelves for imported paperbacks from the U.S./UK. 'What are you doing?' 'One of my books might be here,' she replied, and kept searching. I was very impressed. How marvellous to have your own book on bookshop shelves all over the world! This Angela woman must be the real thing. The bookshop did not carry any of Angela's work in the end, but I told her excitedly, 'Wow! You can look for a copy of your own book in Tokyo, Shinjuku, the opposite side of the globe. It's extraordinary. Like a dream.' Angela beamed. It was the most radiant, happy smile she'd shown me. By then, I knew that Angela had received the Somerset Maugham Award, and had come to Japan with the prize money. A world tour was one of the duties of the prize-winner, but to me, the fact that her book was sold on the other side of the globe sounded far greater, more wonderful, more romantic.

Shinjuku Then

Let me talk about Shinjuku in the sixties and seventies because it's important to say something not only about Angela and me, but also the time and the town.

Shinjuku station in the present-day is vibrant; the east exit is a popular shopping area, the west exit has skyscrapers, and the south exit more shopping areas. Back in the sixties, however, the skyscrapers were just being constructed on the west side, and there was nothing to speak of on the south side. The shopping areas – east and central – measured only a few blocks.

The Kabuki-cho[14] area had already begun to show itself as an entertainment district, though compared to the scale of Kabuki-cho today it was much smaller, and qualitatively different. Sex shops were rare but there were plenty of dance halls, clubs, teahouses, and jazz or classical music cafés. There were places to watch tango live or listen to chanson. The entire size of Shinjuku was perhaps two-thirds, or even half, of its current size.

What really differentiated Shinjuku from the town of today was not its size, but character. Like today, Shinjuku was

Shinjuku in 1970

---

[14] Kabuki-cho: an area in Shinjuku famous for its nightlife activities. Recently the area has become famous for its sex industry.

a busy place, a magnet for the younger generation: students and young office workers. The young people who gathered in this town in the sixties and seventies were very different from today.

In the sixties, the cafés and cheap bars were the haunts of leftish students filled with romanticism and left-wing ideology. They milled around cafés like Fugetsudo and Ramble, or jazz houses like Village Gate, or bars like Donzoko, on a street called Golden-gai. They romanticized anti-establishment ideology, and were caught up in meaningless discussions. Why 'meaningless,' you ask? Because they did not actually believe them: the words, the ideologies (if any) they employed in their discussions. After graduating from university, most of them stopped coming, but instead started working for big corporations – their contribution to the rapid economic growth of Japanese society.

There were future artists as well. They may have used the same jargon of the leftish children but these artists did not waste time. Quite a few had talent and persistence, and they pursued their passions until they established themselves as professional writers, painters, actors, photographers, designers, or musicians and became famous.

Not all of the young customers in these Shinjuku cafés and bars were left-wing students or future artists. In fact, most were there simply because they thought it was fashionable. It was Shinjuku, a 'liberal' town, and they wanted an adventure or a chance encounter, and Shinjuku was the place for easy encounters with strangers. These were the liberal streets that attracted the young hippie fashionista of the 1960s: the so-called '*futen*.'[15]

Among the various kinds of people were young Europeans who travelled around the world on a shoestring. For some reason, they tended to gather at Fugetsudo. If you went there, you could meet Europeans in similar situations and exchange information on surviving in Japan. The Japanese people called them '*furyo gaijin*,'[16] because a small number of away-from-home macho types seduced Japanese girls with crappy lies or took up the dubious marijuana trade. To be fair, of course, there were good foreigners among the Shinjuku regulars.

'I will return to live with you'

In this town of immense scale, disorder, vulgarity, overpowering youth, and vibrancy, Angela and I found each other. There was nothing romantic about it at first. To me, she was just one of the women I encountered on the street, at a café or bar, and with whom I spent a few nights. I supposed she thought the same about me. I thought that, to Angela, an English woman on a world tour on the opposite side of the world, I was just one guy with whom she shared her bed. A curiosity. An adventure.

I did not believe Angela, therefore, when she said to me, 'I will come back to live with you. I'll come back. For sure.' No,

---

[15] *Futen* originally means craziness or a crazy person. In the late sixties, the term was used to describe Shinjuku youths in bell-bottom jeans and funny sunglasses with long hairdos. They tended not to have steady jobs.

[16] A '*furyo gaijin*' literally means a bad foreigner.

I did not think she was lying. I recognized in her words that she was serious, in her own way. But after leaving Japan, she would travel to Southeast Asia and Africa, then return to England, to her everyday life and a husband. I firmly believed that our relationship would become nothing more than a Far East tale, a fond memory, a happening that occurs occasionally and briefly in life. There was no way she would come back all the way to this island in the Far East. To see me? Surely not to live with me.

Letters from Angela started to arrive. The first one was from Hong Kong, I think, the next from Singapore. Enclosed was the paperback she had searched for unsuccessfully in Tokyo, but found at a bookshop in Singapore – *The Magic Toyshop*. It all seemed like a scene in a film, where you spend the night with a woman and then she sends you a book by airmail. I read the book.

The Magic Toyshop was very interesting in parts but also prolix and boring. Now that I think about it, I guess I felt that way not because it had verbose and tedious sections, but because my English was inadequate. The stuff Angela wrote was loaded with flowery words and to be able to fully enjoy her elaborate expressions, your English needed to be superlative. My English level? I was barely able to follow the plot, and could not possibly be entertained by such richness.

I wrote back to Angela with an honest opinion and added what I thought of D.H. Lawrence, whose novel *Lady Chatterley's Lover* I had just read: 'if a writer as dull as he is the greatest English writer of the twentieth century, there are no real authors in England.' The reason for my criticism of dull Lawrence was that, compared to the gamekeeper who possessed intelligence, dignity, and good looks, Lady Chatterley's husband, in spite of wealth and social status, was portrayed as a cowardly weakling. Such stereotypical characterization was worse than a crummy melodrama. I also remember writing that the sex stuff was corny, too.

I read Lawrence because Angela praised him as the greatest British author of the twentieth century. From Angela came the response: 'Essentially, I wrote *The Magic Toyshop* for girls,' and, 'Let's talk about Lawrence when I get back to Japan.'

More letters came. Judging from what Angela wrote, she seemed to think it was a done deal that she would return to Japan.

Chapter 2

Reunion

Around the time I came to know Angela – 1969 to 1970 – I was staying at my brother's place, though not as a lodger. My brother's wife had a serious illness, and they needed someone to take care of their boys, aged one and three, so I stayed at his place and took care of them. My routine in those days was: make lunch for the children and their sick mother, clean the rooms, do the laundry, cook dinner, and take the children to a local park. It occupied half of my day, until one o'clock. Four days a week, I was a private English tutor in the evenings. The rest of the time was mine. I read books and wrote stories. I sent my work to literary contests for newcomers, but the results were always disastrous.

I look back now and think that being young was truly a wonderful thing. I was only twenty-four, invariably cheerful and content. I read Sartre and Capote. I scribbled stories in a dark corner of a café in Shinjuku, and when I got tired, I chatted up a girl. If I struck lucky, I took her to a cheap inn, the sort of place I went with Angela, and had a good time. Just like any other young man. Sometimes I talked with the guys till morning. Guys I hung out with at jazz cafés and bars in Shinjuku.

At the end of a blissful winter came Angela's letter announcing, 'I return to Japan in April.' What did I feel? What did I think when I read Angela's letter? I cannot recall. Most probably, I thought, an English woman writer coming to Japan to see me? No different from a country girl from Nagano or the remote provinces – a girl I'd met in Shinjuku – that was writing to me with, 'I am coming to Tokyo to see you.'

In April of 1970, Angela returned to Japan.[1] I picked her up at Haneda International Airport. It was a gloomy and cold day. There was a passenger waiting area after disembarkation and immigration. I waited. The passengers came down an escalator. I remember just standing, staring up at the escalator, waiting for Angela to appear. My legs were shaking. Not from the excitement at seeing Angela again. I was scared. No, let me be precise. What I felt was much more subtle and complex than that. It was a deeply uncomfortable and uneasy feeling, just like the weather that day, too cold for spring, neither sunshine nor rain. Deep down in my heart was an inexplicable anxiety, best described as an incongruity. It was not the anxiety one feels when facing the unknown, but the kind when facing a situation where you don't know how to react, you don't know what to choose.

Angela came down the escalator in a dress with floral patterns in purple, burgundy, and red. She and her dress looked

---

[1] According to Edmund Gordon's biography of Carter, it was 19 April, 1970 (p.153).

old and uncertain. When she saw me, she smiled an awkward, forced smile. She looked terrified, just as I was. She was probably bound up in the same inexplicable feeling of apprehension. My memory of that day is patchy and dreamlike. Angela was sitting on a bench in a lobby-like place, talking to an elderly Japanese man. I sat down beside her and took her hand. It was warm. We were intimate. We were talking, but the old man would not stop jabbering to Angela. She turned to me, and as if to make an excuse, said, 'It's because I have a gentle face.' To be sure, Angela did look like a kind nursery school teacher – Aunty Angela – nodding to the old guy. 'Let's go.' I said a couple of words to him, and grabbed Angela's suitcase. Seeing Angela stand up, the old man mumbled something and extended his hand, which Angela shook, and replied smiling.

We took a taxi and went to Shibuya, where we checked into a hotel; something between a business hotel and a *tsurekomi*. We must have talked a lot in the taxi. I remember nothing – what we said, how she was. We went into the hotel room. I glanced at a painting on the wall and looked out the window. Angela mumbled something, but I couldn't hear. She sat in the chair cross-legged, watching me. 'It's strange. Don't you think?' Her violet eyes and her gentle, cool glance gave me a funny feeling. It was like a Hollywood film. I took off my clothes slowly, first my jeans and underpants. I already had a hard-on (I was so young). I announced, 'You came back for this.' Such a lame line from a cheap porno film or a novel. It sounded so childish. Yet, when I look back, it was perfect. My silly performance worked a miracle. It shattered the awkward tension. Glancing at my prick that was abruptly offered for her inspection, Angela said, 'Hm. Partly yes,' then added, 'but not just that.' A light flickered in her eyes. It excited my desire and erotic imagination. Her face suddenly lit up. It bloomed with vigour and allure, a stark contrast to the face a moment before. Then she was a tired, middle-aged woman. It was nervousness that made her look older than she was, turning her into an dull, middle-aged, housewifely thing.

We made love straightaway and that drew us close again. Holding each other, we talked about many things. Angela said she had separated from her husband, who had a young girlfriend. I told her, 'During these six months' time, I slept with ten women and wrote two novel-like pieces.' The number of conquests was a boast. 'What do you mean "novel-like pieces"?' asked Angela. I answered, 'Well, I want to think of them as novels but they probably don't deserve that name.' Angela said, 'You need to have more confidence in what you write. That's the first step.'

'Confidence? Never had such a thing.'

'I thought you were full of self-esteem.'

'That's just a facade. To those who don't know me well, I'm an arrogant bastard.'

I was half joking, but in retrospect, it was a confession of my inner feelings. 'You must have confidence. Without it, you'll never get anywhere,' Angela persisted. I replied to her in my head, 'But look at you. You always look so unsure.'

Angela never looked certain or confident. Certainly not

when we first met. Not the morning we slept together for the first time. Not during our rendezvous. Not the day we reunited after half a year. On the contrary, she always looked timid and nervous. She gave off the atmosphere of a shy schoolgirl who was interested only in literature, a girl disproportionately mature in her head but unable to socialize with others.

The Flat in Meguro

The next day, we started looking for a flat for Angela. Finding a residence for a foreigner was a weird and awkward experience in 1970. I doubt the situation has changed much since. In a matter-of-fact fashion, I took her to a downtown realtor and said to the middle-aged man at the table, 'Hi, we're looking for a flat.' He answered rudely, 'Who? You? Who's the occupant? You? That foreigner?' 'Yes, this lady,' I answered politely. 'The foreigner! That's going to be difficult. They don't understand the language,' he said. I tried to fend off his worries, saying, 'I can come by if you need me. Just give me a call, and I'll come at once.' The man's frigid expression did not alter. He continued, 'Us and foreigners. We're different. Different customs. Ok, I know one place. Let me make a phone call.' He made us sit down and started calling, but after a while, put down the phone. 'Just as I thought. They don't take foreigners. Foreigners don't understand what we say. Different customs.' His face did not change.

We visited another realtor immediately. This time, I went in without Angela. The realtor hesitated, but the result was still the same. The negotiation was going fine until they realized the actual tenant was an English woman. Then the negotiation collapsed: 'They don't understand our language. Their customs are different.' We went on to other places. There was not even one flat Angela could rent.

That evening, we dined at a *yakitori*[2] restaurant. We wondered how foreigners ever found places to live in Tokyo. Angela said, 'There may be a realtor that specializes in foreigners.' 'Yes, that must be it!' I said. It was still baffling and unreasonable. I could not understand why they needed to differentiate – foreigner and Japanese – in such a simple matter as renting a flat. Then it hit me: 'As soon as they see a foreigner, a Caucasian in particular, Japanese think they have to speak English. That's the problem. At Fugetsudo or Shinjuku jazz cafés, they get on just fine with foreign customers. The employees don't try to speak in English to foreign guests. Whether understood or not, they speak to them, take orders, and give instructions in Japanese – the way it should be. If you have to speak to foreigners in English, you can't do business with them. It's contradictory.' As I was repeating my analysis, Angela suddenly beamed and with that charming smile that was so much her own, announced, 'I know a place. It'll be solved tomorrow.'

That night, we stayed at a *tsurekomi*. It was a passionate night, with the sound of our neighbours' sexual ecstasies filtering through the thin wall as background music.

The next morning, Angela went somewhere, leaving me

---

[2] *Yakitori* is a Japanese dish of charcoal-grilled chicken on skewers.

behind. In the afternoon, we met again in Shinjuku, in front of Kinokuniya as planned, and headed for Meguro. At the Meguro exit a small man in a black suit was waiting for us. He spoke in broken English. After a seven or eight minute brisk walk, he led us to a detached house with two flats on the ground floor and two upstairs. At the entrance hung three nameplates: foreign names. A vacant apartment in a budget tenement for people from overseas.

Angela took the back flat on the ground floor. It was as small as six *tatami* mats, and looked even smaller than that. It had a kitchen, a bathroom and, conveniently, a telephone line. The monthly rent was 40,000 yen. The man told me, 'You can't find a flat cheaper than this, anywhere.' When Angela was away, he whispered to me, 'Is it true this woman's an author? Writers earn a stack, don't they? Seicho Matsumoto's[3] annual income's over 20 million, right?'

Earlier that morning, Angela had made a phone call to either the British Council or the British Embassy, asking them for help, telling them she was in urgent need of a place to live.[4] They introduced her to a volunteer organization that offered support to British citizens living in Tokyo. This led to a real estate broker doing business with foreigners, and to the flat in Meguro. All so smooth and easy. Apparently, there was a foreigners-only network that ordinary Japanese were not

---

[3] Seicho Matsumoto: a popular novelist specializing in mysteries.
[4] Apparently, Carter hated solely depending on Sozo, and letting him control her housing situation. See Gordon, p. 154.

aware of, providing everyday help to each other. Just three days had elapsed since Angela returned to Japan and through her I learned about the invisible wall in Japanese society that barred foreigners, as well as the invisible network exclusive to foreigners. Later, these things would create a dramatic, gaping chasm between Angela and me.

I had not remotely expected to set up with Angela when she came back to Japan. Not that I did not want to. But the possibility of living with Angela never occurred to me. When I uttered nothing decisive, Angela insisted ever more urgently she should live with me: 'I came back to Japan to live in the same place as you,' and repeated, 'There's no point in my staying in Japan if I can't live with you.' I thought Angela suspected I had a girlfriend, that I saw her and spent nights together with her. Naturally, her suspicions were not totally unfounded. They were, substantially, reality. In those days, however, though I regularly seduced girls at cafés or bars and had one-night stands, I never launched a serious relationship with anyone. Looking back now, it makes me wonder. Why did I not get seriously involved with any of the girls I slept with? They were all sort of pretty and good-natured. The truth is, I think now, I was a terribly immature twenty-five year old, incapable of any form of a serious relationship with women, even as friends, much less as a girlfriend.

The night Angela signed the contract for the flat, we stayed one more night at the same *tsurekomi* as the previous day. Angela's strong will finally had its way. It was as if I was being swept away by a strong current. I decided to live with

Angela, but in my mind, it was not a big deal. I simply let the matter take its course, and it happened just so. And so it came about that life with Angela began in a small flat in Meguro (a good size for a young person in those days).

Looking back, I know I was unbelievably spineless and hideously irresponsible. To myself, to Angela. As for Angela? How thoughtless, optimistic, and fearless. Wanting to live with a man she barely knew… Angela and I were both young. That's what it all meant. Being young, being reckless, optimistic, and fearless, just like we were.

Japanese Language Lessons

My everyday routine was as follows: go to my brother's house twice a week to do the cleaning, laundry, cooking, and shopping for his bedridden wife. Take the children to a nearby park, then off to my job as a private tutor. After my work finished, I would go to Shinjuku for a coffee at Fugetsudo or someplace else, then head back to the flat in Meguro where Angela was waiting for me. I tried to consume as many books as possible during childcare time and when on the train. I also continued to pen some novel-like pieces at cafés.

At first, Angela stayed in the flat while I was out and about. Then she quickly got a job checking English for NHK[5] TV international broadcasting. According to Angela, she had little to do. The English of the NHK employees was practically

---

[5] NHK: short form for Nihon Hoso Kyokai, the only national broadcasting company in Japan.

flawless, so she whiled away her time reading books. 'They hired me,' she said, 'just to make sure their English was fine.' Thanks to NHK, Angela read quite a few books on Japan. An NHK employee once told Angela, 'People will respect you if you say you're working for NHK.' This made Angela laugh, but was true. People reacted better when she said she worked 'for NHK' than when she said she was 'a writer.'

She received this plum job, with time to herself, through the same network that helped her find the flat – a grapevine only visible and open to foreigners (or rather, Europeans and Americans). There was nothing I could do to help Angela find a room or a job. I was merely there as her conversational companion over tea or coffee, or beer, and her lover in bed. It was a less than ideal relationship, and it urged me to think of a way I could help her. To prove how useful I could be. So, I started teaching her Japanese.

I first tried to teach *hiragana*, the Japanese alphabet.[6] 'A, I, U, E, O, KA, KI, KU, KE, KO....' reading each sound aloud, trying to get Angela to grasp the peculiar shapes of *hiragana*. I taught her the 50 *hiragana* characters in this way. I bought a picture book for small children and we recited the *hiragana* together. It was exactly the same method used for teaching kindergarten.

To my surprise, Angela showed no curiosity in *hiragana*. She made no comment on their peculiar configuration. She read them – stammering – when I read them aloud and made

---

[6] *Hiragana*: a basic component of the system of written Japanese. A syllabary.

her repeat, but it all seemed grudging, for my sake, because I was making an effort. In fact, she seemed irritated.

When she could cope fairly well with *hiragana*, I started teaching her basic phrases. I firmly believed that the mystery of the Japanese language could hardly fail to grab her interest.

First, I went through the basic structural differences between Japanese and English. 'When you want to say, "He went to Shinjuku to see a friend yesterday" in Japanese, you start with "he," and after that, translate in reverse order. Then you'll get it right most of the time. *Kare wa, kinou, tomodachi ni ai ni Shinjuku e itta.*[7] See? Japanese sentences and English sentences are, quite literally, in the opposite order.'

'And in most cases Japanese nouns have no plural. "*Hon*" (book) is always "*hon*" (book or books). "*Inu*" (dog) is just "*inu*," no matter how many creatures. Most of the time, we specify neither subject nor object, unless it is unusually difficult to speculate what they are from the context. For example, when you want to say, "I love you," you just say "Love" (*Sukida*)."[8] Neither "I" nor "you" are necessary, because, when you say "*Sukida*" to someone right in front of you, it's obvious who you love. Right?'

'If you want to ask, "Where are you going?" you say,

---

[7] This sentence can be translated word for word, 'He, yesterday, friend, to see, to Shinjuku, went.' The word, '*tomodachi*' can mean both 'a friend' and 'friends' as the author tells the reader in the following part.

[8] '*Suki*' literally translates to the verb 'love,' and '*da*' suggests the speaker is a male.

[9] It literally translates to 'where go?'

"Where go? (*Doko ikuno*?)"[9] "What are you going to eat?" becomes "What eat? (*Nani taberu*?)"[10] But depending on the context, "*Nani taberu*?" can also mean, "What shall we eat?" Situation dictates the meaning and that invites frequent misunderstandings. But nobody really cares, except for special cases, like legal matters.'

'What's more difficult is the difference between polite Japanese for business situations and casual Japanese used among friends and family. We have three kinds of honorific diction, 'honorary,' 'polite,' and 'modest,' and it's very hard to have a good command of them. You need a certain level of education, intelligence, and experience. Few Japanese are confident in their usage. In fact, most of us speak imperfect Japanese.'

While I was saying these things, I jotted down some things in the alphabet and *hiragana* to summarize. Judging from the expression on her face, I knew Angela understood most of what I said. However, she would not try to memorize the basic Japanese words and phrases I wrote in the booklet. When I read them aloud and made her repeat them, she would mumble them once or twice, then stand up saying, 'I'm going to make coffee,' then leave for the kitchen.

Though she showed almost zero interest in the Japanese language, she was suddenly intrigued when I commented, 'In the Japanese language, male and female vocabulary are subtly different. It sounds strange when a man uses a female word, and it is equally strange when a woman uses a male word.' She said, 'That's not good. That kind of gender difference in speech must be the cause of such extreme discrimination against women in Japan. No?' Then she launched eloquently into the topic of gender bias in Japan. Most of it was regurgitated from books she had read, not first-hand experience. This doesn't mean she was wrong.

Anyway, I gave up on teaching Angela Japanese. I was truly surprised, not only by the fact that she was not keen to learn Japanese, but that she had zero interest in the language itself. Personally, I think when you are interested in another country and want to know more, you study the language. It's essential, effective. It is tough, and you need not be an expert, but it is neither meaningless to memorize words and phrases. Trivial expressions and words reveal much about a country's unique culture, its tradition, thought, and sensibilities buried deep within.

For instance, the Japanese use four types of writing: Chinese characters, *hiragana*, *katakana*,[11] and the Roman alphabet. They allow us to use particular forms in a certain context, though the difference is extremely subtle. I believe that this writing system resulted in *'manga,'* which exhibits an overabundant sensitivity to signs. You could also say that the omission of subjects and objects, or the way a conclusion is painstakingly deferred in Japanese conversational language, might reflect the subconscious desire of Japanese people to dilute self-assertion as much as possible in order to avoid con-

---

[11] Another kind of syllabary in the Japanese writing system. It is used often for imported words, and onomatopoeia.

flicts, and so on....

'Setsunai'

Was Angela uninterested in Japanese culture? On the contrary, she read Japanese literature extensively, from the classics to the contemporary, in English translation. She also read books on social issues, such as the issue of *burakumin* discrimination,[12] and psychosocial theories, such as 'the logic of a vertically structured society.'

She did not remain a purely academic observer of Japan, but rather she formed her own unique opinion and value judgment. Every artist does. Here, I will try to write down some of her verdicts on Japanese writers. Interestingly, she slugged Yukio Mishima,[13] popular among foreigners, in one fell blow, saying, 'He's a shallow writer without any real talent. And he poses as a heterosexual even though he's not.'[14] This was contrary to the general opinion on Mishima.

With Osamu Dazai,[15] she was adamantly displeased: 'His childish manner is nauseating. A typical Japanese man. Horrendous immaturity.' She actually threw his *No Longer Human* at the wall when she was reading it.

---

[12] The word '*burakumin*' is usually used to indicate the discriminated groups of people supposedly descended from the lowest rung of the pre-modern social structure. Though this type of discrimination was banned in the Meiji era, it still remains unresolved in Japanese society.

[13] Yukio Mishima (1925-1970): a male Japanese author whose avant-garde works, including *The Temple of the Golden Pavillion* and *Forbidden Colors*, were internationally renowned. He committed ritual suicide by *hara-kiri* after the failure of his coup d'état.

She showed no interest in Kenzaburo Oe[16] either, saying, 'Embraces narcissism, and not a shred of sexiness.'

On the other hand, she guardedly praised Kobo Abe:[17] 'He's phony but has interesting ideas, and as a mystery writer, is first class.'

To my surprise, she spoke highly of *The Pornographers* written by Akiyuki Nosaka.[18] She said, 'Nosaka will be praised in the future and rated highly, even by overseas readers.'

She had a great admiration for Jun'ichiro Tanizaki's[19] *Some*

---

[14] In an interview, Carter says, "Well, reading his novels is like being on a train with someone very unpleasant, like being on a train with a compulsive madman, and he starts a conversation with you and he goes on and on and on, and he starts telling you about himself and he tells you how he first masturbated when he was eleven and he realized it was terribly wicked and how his grandmother used to hit on the ceiling with a stick and it used to frighten him very much because he masturbated and his voice gets, you know, more and more and more and more agitated and his hand, he starts pawing you with his hot hands and his hot breath is blasting in your face and…well, he's forcing you to listen to this very, well, really rather adolescent…well, *Angst*" (Ronald Bell, ed., *The Japan Experience*, Weatherhill, 1973, pp.34-35.)

[15] Osamu Dazai (1909-1948): a male Japanese author with the internationally acclaimed *The Setting Sun* and *No Longer Human*. Noted for his irony. Killed himself after many unsuccessful attempts at suicide.

[16] Kenzaburo Oe (1935-2015): a Nobel Prize winning author and a major figure in contemporary Japanese literature.

[17] Kobo Abe (1924-1993): a male Japanese author renowned for his Kafkaesque nightmarish fictional world. His *Woman in the Dunes* is particularly well known.

[18] Akiyuki Nosaka (1930-2015): a less famous Japanese writer compared to others mentioned in this section. *The Pornographers* was his first novel, after which he published *Grave of the Fireflies* and *American Hiziki* to wide acclaim. He has been more active as an essay writer than as a novelist.

[19] See page 16-17.

Prefer Nettles, *Diary of a Mad Old Man*, and *The Makioka Sisters*, saying they were 'super.' She liked the *Diary of a Mad Old Man* especially, and considered him to be one of the greatest authors, comparable to Dostoyevsky and D.H. Lawrence. She also valued him highly as a philosopher with philosophical ideas similar to Freud, of whom she was an ardent admirer.[20]

It took me by surprise when she spoke highly of Soseki Natsume.[21] She called him 'a very agreeable old man with considerable intelligence.' She often recommended him to her British friends or other Caucasian friends, saying, 'He's a very interesting philosopher, as well as a writer of fiction. Soseki Natsume should be read more widely in England and in Europe.'

Among classical literature, *The Tale of Genji*[22] earned high

---

[20] Carter says in an interview, 'I think Tanizaki is one of the world's great novelists. He is partly because he knew what he was writing about. I think that his work is all about the great confrontation – or the mini-confrontation, depending on which end of the telescope you're looking though – between East and West. But that was his thing, he was writing about a changing morality, I think. And part of his genious was that he wrote about this changing morality without ever telling you that he was: he didn't dot the i's and cross the t's, if you know what I mean' (Ronald Bell, ed., *The Japan Experience*, Weatherhill, 1973, p. 34).

[21] Soseki Natsume (1867-1916): one of the foremost Japanese authors in the Meiji period. He is best known for *Kokoro*, *Botchan*, and *I am Cat*. He was also a scholar of British literature, and was sent to England to study. His work reflects the influence of Western culture, as well as his ambivalence toward it, which led him to explore Japanese-ness in his fiction.

[22] *The Tale of Genji* is said to be the world's first novel, written in the early eleventh century (during the Heian period) by a Japanese noblewoman, Murasaki Shikibu. It is a story of a beautiful aristocrat, Genji, and his women and children. The first complete English translation was done by Edward Seidensticker in 1976.

regard. I learned from her that Murasaki Shikibu was called 'Lady Purple' in English. The concept of '*mono no aware*'[23] became the topic of our conversation several times, but as far as I can remember, Angela never grasped what it meant. To tell the truth, I myself did not know what it was and still do not. When I said, 'I don't really know what it means,' she never brought it up again. Perhaps she was relieved by my confession. Or she just gave up.

Instead of '*mono no aware*,' I taught her the expression, '*setsunai*,'[24] a sentiment more intimately felt by today's Japanese. The expression '*setsunai*' was so familiar to me even I was able to explain it. Angela took a liking to '*setsunai*,' and used it frequently while we were together. Finding a pretty flower by the road, watching a Japanese romantic movie, or watching the setting sun, she often said '*setsunai*.'

Though she found Basho Matsuo,[25] the author of *Oku no Hosomichi* (*The Narrow Road to the Deep North*), an interesting old geezer, calling him 'a hippie,' his world of '*wabi*' and '*sabi*' stimulated her curiosity only superficially. On the other

---

[23] '*Mono no aware*': a Japanese term to describe the transience of things and the sad appreciation of passing things. The renowned Japanese scholar of the Edo period, Norinaga Motoori, used this term to describe the general atmosphere of the *Tale of Genji*.

[24] '*Setsunai*': a Japanese adjective to describe something painfully and romantically sad, or heart-rending.

[25] Basho Matsuo (1644-1694): the most famous poet of the Edo period in Japan. He is internationally recognized as the master of haiku.

[26] Issa Kobayashi (1763-1828): though less known internationally, he is considered to be one of the four masters of *haiku*, along with Basho, Buson, and Shiki.

hand, when she came across the *haiku* of Issa Kobayashi,[26] she was greatly pleased, and praised these *haiku*. 'So cute!' So charming!' she would exclaim, slapping her knees with her hands in delight. Looking back, I kind of belatedly begin to understand the sensibilities of Angela Carter.

Angela was also interested in *manga*, fascinated by its grotesque visualization, and whenever she got tired of reading or writing, she would copy the pictures from *manga* into her notebook.

She was not at all taken by Zen Buddhism. To some, this may be surprising. To others, typical of her. I recommended a book on Zen written by Daisetsu Suzuki[27] and she devoured it in one go. She said, 'It puts far too much emphasis on intuition and lacks logic. This must well explain why the Japanese plunged into World War II. The result of sheer stupidity.' Her outright disregard of Zen much amused me, because I had thought every intellectual elite from abroad was interested, or at least pretended to be interested, in Zen. She showed little interest in the religious aspects of Japanese culture, but found the roadside *jizo*[28] statues intriguing. She called them 'charming' and patted their heads.

---

[27] Daisetsu Suzuki (1870-1966): some call him the most important scholar of Buddhism in modern Japan. He wrote many books on Zen in English. Known as D. T. Suzuki globally.

[28] *Jizo*: originally a bodhisattva, Ksitigharba, a Buddhist monk revered primarily in East Asia. In Japan, he was one of the most popular gods, affectionately called, *'Ojizo-sama,'* Traditionally, he is believed to be the guardian of children who died before their parents, or unborn fetuses. His statue is commonly seen on roadsides or in graveyards.

Judeo-Christian Culture

From the very beginning, Angela frequently used the term, 'Judeo-Christian culture' or 'the Judeo-Christian world,' to describe England and Europe as a whole. Back then, I thought 'Christian culture' would suffice, and I did not understand why she had to add 'Judeo-.' It sounded odd, strange. It did not occur to me that Judaism and Jewish culture were so interwoven with Christianity. Of course, I knew that the Old Testament was also the scripture of Judaism, but I did not realize the impact of a book full of parables on the glorious European culture that produced Newton, John Locke, and Darwin.

To Japanese, I think, Genesis seemed like another simple myth about the origin of Earth commonly found anywhere. The tale of Moses seemed a childish fantasy. I could not understand how grown-up people in the twentieth century could talk seriously about 'God's punishment,' or 'sins,' or 'retribution.'

Certainly, I was aware that the Christian concept of God held significant status in Western art, music, literature, and philosophy, but I thought also that such a concept was a straight up façade. Did anyone really believe in it? I assumed few, if any. When I was young, faith seemed like a barrel of laughs, a powerless thing in the real world.

(Recently, I had an inspirational conversation with a Christian missionary. This young missionary, in his thirties, said to me, 'Faith doesn't mean to believe in what you imagine it to be. It is to pretend to believe in what you cannot, and to spend every day according to that pretence. That is faith.' Now that I can grasp. Maybe.)

Angela was not actively Christian, but she believed in the power of Judaism and Christianity. She felt that the cradle of Western culture in England, Europe, and the U.S. was Judeo-Christianity and, therefore, Western people were prepossessed with the Judeo-Christian concepts of sin and punishment. This made them culturally exceptional in the world.

She thought of Japan as being integrated by its own morality, and believed that its philosophy of life and view of the world were totally different, because Japan had not been contaminated by Judaism or Christianity. Her idea was somewhat similar to Ruth Benedict's *The Chrysanthemum and the Sword*,[29] though Angela's view was more extreme. She regarded Japanese culture as frankly mysterious.

Angela's ideas sounded terribly childish. I frequently told her, 'Look. They may sound different from Christian notions but Japanese ideas aren't that different, okay? In Japan you get punished when you murder or steal, just as in the Christian world. Sexual liberty is not appreciated. You're praised when you listen to your seniors and you do good things for others… Essentially, there isn't much difference, is there?' Angela would not listen to me, however. She insisted on her own theory, citing extreme examples of a world dominated by Judeo-Christianity. She used hideously complicated vocabulary so I

---

[29] Ruth Benedict was an American anthropologist and cultural relativist whose major work, *The Chrysanthemum and the Sword*, a study on Japanese society and culture, was published in 1946.

could not follow her argument. It seemed to me she was talking to herself, persuading herself rather than me.

I think that it was probably important to her that her culture be odd or exceptional, no matter good or bad. Presumably, she couldn't bear the thought that she and her world were commonplace, and could be found anywhere on earth. The world Angela belonged to had to be an incomparably tragic one. It had to be distorted and tortured by the overpowering dictatorship of Judaism and Christianity. To think of her culture as just something quite ordinary would have reduced her to a colourless creature robbed of glamour. For Angela, what was important, more than anything else, was to be glamourous. It followed that being peculiar, being exceptional, was the basic condition for that glamour.

I regarded Angela's types of ideas as neither peculiar nor exceptional, though Angela would have been terribly upset to hear that. No matter what period of time, or where in the world you go, you see obnoxious people with ideas like hers. Of course, Tokyo in those days had more than its fair share of people who wanted to insist on their exceptionalism and particularity.

Along with such sensibilities, Angela also propounded a theory of sexuality that at the time sounded new to me. She said that everyone in the West, contaminated by Judeo-Christianity, was possessed with a massive sense of guilt about life in general. They were deeply repressed, especially with regard to sexuality. They were neither liberal nor liberated. Contrary to the West, she believed the Japanese were not under the control of Judaism or Christianity, and that they enjoyed sexuality to their heart's content.

The general view of the Japanese about their own sexuality was the reverse of Angela's. We thought that compared to the repressed Japanese people, Westerners were sexually liberal and liberated and that they indeed enjoyed richer sex lives.

Now putting aside the question of whether or not the Japanese were really free and liberated, Angela certainly was herself repressed, to a degree, in sexual matters. Was it this repression that prevented Angela from perceiving the tactics employed by women to seduce men?

For instance, she did not understand how a woman might look and behave rigid and chaste on the surface, but could seduce a man sexually in a subtle, inconspicuous, and delicate way. Angela seemed to view seduction merely as what a stripper does on stage in front of a male audience. Our everyday life does not provide us with such a stage, and Angela would not know how to act like a stripper anyhow. She lacked training. As a result, she did not know how to seduce a man.

Sexual matters between men and women might have seemed to Angela at that time a mysterious terrain beyond an inscrutable haze. She caught a glimpse now and then, but it never revealed itself to her in the entirety. Perhaps that was why she found relationships between men and women, with sex at their core, inexhaustibly intriguing and so appealing. It may also explain, partly, why her stories are flecked with so many twisted sexual fantasies.

Chapter 3

My Inferiority Complex toward Caucasians

Angela and I began to live together in a small apartment, located in a slightly impoverished residential area five or six minutes from Meguro station. To me, my life with her felt very natural. It may surprise many readers, but I felt almost no differences in culture or habits while living with Angela. (To tell the truth, I felt such differences more acutely when I started to live with a Japanese woman after I separated from Angela.)

We had never discussed it, but we shared responsibility in cooking, cleaning, washing, shopping, and other house chores, and each of us paid about half of the living costs. We sat facing each other on *tatami* mats, with a small dining table we had bought in an antique shop between us, and talked with each other all the time while eating food or drinking tea. I enjoyed asking questions to Angela, listening to what she had to say, challenging her sometimes or starting again with a new set of questions and answers. I am sure Angela enjoyed it, too: to listen to my ideas, to ask me questions, to hear what I had to say, and to make comments, agreeing or disagreeing with me. We talked about anything and everything, from politics to pop music.

One of the topics I repeatedly talked with Angela about was how much the Japanese had learned from the English. To put it simply, we owe the system of democracy itself to the English. I, personally, was greatly influenced by John Locke and John Stuart Mill. I told her many times how much I admired Mill's utilitarianism in particular, with its general principle that what is useful and beneficial is also good and legitimate.

I still think Mill's principle is important, forty years later. Even in a twenty-first century capitalist society that is supposed to be free from doctrines, we are in fact bound by various 'ism's, both old and new, which keep us from objective judgment, disabling our thinking and our lives. All we need to really do is evaluate things level-headedly by their usefulness.

While praising English civilization, I also frequently said to Angela that because the English had conquered and colonized the world, they, or the Anglo-Saxons, were the people the Asians and Africans wanted most to overthrow and make taste defeat. To such an antiquated remark, Angela would cast me an ironic look mixed with curiosity and pity, saying, 'The glory of Great Britain is long gone, you know. You don't need to say such a thing, because this is already the era of Asian dominance.'

Another thing I said to her often was, 'If you were a Mexican or a Venezuelan woman with Native American blood, I could have loved you more without reservation.' It was a silly thing to say, but I was not totally joking then. Through me,

Angela was probably able to sense a troubled and contradictory Asian mentality.

I truly enjoyed the time I spent with Angela whenever we talked like this in our small flat or at a nearby café. I knew Angela enjoyed her time with me, too. We encountered many surprises because of our different cultural backgrounds, and they served only to increase our happiness. I firmly believe that happiness did not stem merely from a shallow place. Even now, after forty years, I can definitely say that we had a profound understanding of each other. We had so much in common, had a deep interest in each other, stimulated each other's minds. Both felt for, and yet fought against, the other at an incredibly deep level.

The good times, however, were limited to the time we spent alone with each other. When we left our little bubble of seclusion and mingled with others, the situation changed dramatically.

I did not introduce Angela to any of my friends or my mates from the pub until we had been living together for two or three weeks. When they learned that I was living with a British woman, they became so curious that they urged me to introduce her to them. But I was reluctant for some reason. Now that I think about it, honestly, I am not sure why. Angela was not at all fashion conscious – she put little to no make-up on, and most of the time wore jeans with a shirt and a jacket. She was thirty years old then, but looked about thirty-five if you compared her to Japanese women. To twenty-something young men, she may have looked almost middle-aged. The girls in Tokyo spent an exorbitant amount of energy and effort on fashion in order to look beautiful, appealing, and younger than reality. In comparison to them, Angela did not possess such qualities that an average Japanese man would want in a woman, and so she would not have excited their sexual desire. Was that the reason behind my reluctance?

Angela was not at all overweight, though. She was tall and slender. Her face could be described as handsome, and she had an abundance of chestnut hair that was very attractive. She was a good-looking woman, as I recall now. Some of the Hollywood actresses in these past twenty years or so look rather like Angela. So what made me hesitate to introduce her to my mates?

It was extremely silly of me, but deep down in my heart, I held Elizabeth Taylor and Vivien Leigh as the ideal images for white women. Stupidly enough, I felt a bit ashamed to have a white girlfriend who did not live up to the full-blown womanly charm of those actresses. I was embarrassed for friends to see me being pleased with a white girlfriend who was not exactly a peerless beauty. I could not bear the thought that my friends would regard me as a silly flirt, having fallen in love with a woman only because she was white.[1] At that time, my mind was dominated by such immature thoughts about race and culture.

---

[1] Although Araki calls it racism, I, the translator, think this part shows the typical insular mentality and homosociality of Japanese society, in which what matters to a man is how he is judged by other men.

An Arrogant American Man

Angela, on the other hand, wanted to introduce me to her British and American friends that she had become acquainted with in Tokyo. She wanted, and expected, me to make friends with the foreigners she had met, because I spoke English a little and was sociable enough. Of course, it was only natural of her to expect this.

I did not refuse when Angela invited me to meet foreign acquaintances of hers. I thought it was going to be fun to meet and chat with them. However, when I first met an American man in his fifties with a rather atavistic appearance at a restaurant in Shibuya, I realized that it was not going to be as simple as I had imagined. The American man was in the business of creating and supervising English language education materials, and was accompanied that night by a young Japanese woman who did not speak English well. With a permanent smile plastered across her face, she whispered something to the American man, who in turn said something back in broken Japanese. The woman uttered practically nothing after that; she only kept smiling. She was one of the typical Japanese girls in those days who would only date foreign men. My friends scornfully branded those girls as *'gaisen'* (foreigner specialists).

From the moment I laid my eyes on him, I sensed something very disagreeable about this middle-aged American man. He was strangely arrogant, in spite of his less-than-impressive appearance. He did not even look at me when I joked to him, as if he had not heard me. Looking back now, he was one of the nasty Americans out and about in those days who exhibited an overbearing air, only because their country had been victorious in the war.

When I talked about him a few days later, Angela tried to defend him by saying that he was probably displeased to see me, a Japanese man much younger than himself, with her, when he had been looking forward to having a proper chat with a reasonable white woman at last. Angela added, 'You made him jealous because you're so beautiful.' I was not convinced.

Anyway, the four of us sat at a table in a restaurant in Shibuya and started eating our awkward dinner. Angela merely greeted the Japanese girl and utterly ignored her afterwards, chattering away with the American man. Come to think of it, Angela was not particularly attentive to other's feelings. Like many other Europeans and Americans, particularly women, she only paid attention to those, even Japanese women, who could assert themselves in English, and ignored those who could not. It suggested her tactlessness, but in my opinion it was also foolishness and coldness. Taking this tendency of hers into account, it seems only natural to me that she easily made friends with Europeans and Americans, but had difficulties with the Japanese.

I was abruptly thrown into a difficult position. Angela and the American man were having a good time, busily talking and joking with each other. Angela frequently urged me to join them, but alas, with my poor English I was barely able to follow what they were saying. The American chap deliberately and completely ignored me. The Japanese girl in front of me wore the same smile, clinging to the arm of her American boyfriend. She seemed quite accustomed to situations like this.

In cases such as this, I now realize it would be best to talk enthusiastically and take control of the conversation. Unfortunately, with my age, status, and language competency, I dared not try that method. Drinking beer stone-faced did not seem nice, either, so there was not much else to do except simper meaninglessly from time to time.

That awkward inactivity lasted quite a while. I started to feel unbearably restless from a doubt that nagged at me. How did I look to other Japanese people around me? I became convinced that I was seen as an unpleasant Japanese youngster who was foolish enough to be delighted to be around white people, even though he did not understand English well, meekly playing a Japanese goody-two-shoes to flatter them.

It was unthinkable for me to initiate a conversation with the Japanese girl sitting obediently next to the American chap. If I enjoyed talking with her, I would run the risk of being taken as the same colonised subject as she was, who, in spite of her inability to speak their language, was trying her best to please the coloniser.

I became so impossibly self-conscious I was close to exploding. I had to quickly make up my mind as to what my next action would be. After a while, I rose to my feet saying, 'Excuse me.' I leaned aside and told Angela, 'I'm bored stiff.

I'm going to the bar over there to have some cocktails,' and left the table to go to the bar at the back.

I had a martini at the bar, but felt absurd drinking alone, so I decided to go to Shinjuku. I returned to the table and told Angela that I was going to Shinjuku, then purposely said to the American man, 'Nice meeting you, I'll see you again,' before leaving the restaurant. While in Shinjuku, I went to a few bars where I thought I might find my drinking buddies, and having found the usual faces at Donzoko, I drank there again before heading back to the Meguro flat around midnight.

Donzoko today

Angela was home already, and we started quarrelling immediately. It was our first real argument. Angela said to me that I was being childish and naïve, and by this, she meant I did not know the real world. Angela was right to call me such things, but putting that aside, the real problem was solely that

I did not have a good command of English. If I had been more fluent, I could have teased the American chap and his Japanese girlfriend with a comment loaded with sarcasm, such as, 'The two of you remind me of the American soldiers and the Japanese prostitutes we called "pan-pan." I used to see them around town during my childhood. Those were the good ol' days!' Unfortunately, I was not skilful enough to pilot myself through the conversation between Angela and the man to bring forth such cutting remarks.

These things were certainly on my mind, but I did not tell them to Angela. Instead, I said somewhat theatrically, 'The problem isn't that I'm childish or naïve, but rather I shouldn't have sat at his table to begin with. If I'd met him at Fugetsudo, I probably would have thrown some nasty remarks at him, like, "Where did you pick up that pussycat?" I would never, ever sit at the same table as him.' Looking back, I do not think I was keen to discuss with anyone, not even with Angela, the humiliating scenes I used to witness in my childhood of American soldiers and Japanese prostitutes.[2]

Angela said to me, 'I want to have pride in my man. Why don't you behave like a respectable grown-up?' I retorted, 'That sounds like a quote from a Hollywood film.' Then she

---

[2] This episode with the American man shows the complex feelings of Japanese men in postwar era, though Araki seems unaware of it. The loss of World War Ⅱ was experienced by them as a humiliating effemination, a sort of castration. Seeing a Japanese woman having a sexual relationship with an American man was doubly humiliating in the patriarchal way of thinking, as they felt that they were robbed of their own property that they should have retained ownership of.

said in an even more dramatic tone, 'Life is not like a Marlon Brando film, or a novel by Dostoyevsky. Grow up!' To be honest, in those days, I would often imitate characters from Marlon Brando films or from the stories of Dostoyevsky. I was not the only one, however. Even Angela, when she started to mingle with Japanese friends of mine, acted like Blanche in *A Streetcar Named Desire*. Though in her case, it was not a deliberate act. Angela could not help but behave like Vivien Leigh in that role.

Her Phobia of the Japanese

After about three weeks into our life together, I took Angela to meet my mates from the pub in Shinjuku. I still remember when I met up with Angela at Shinjuku station. She was walking among crowds of Japanese people at the concourse. How tall she looked, and how beautiful her legs were. I was impressed all over again.

When we arrived at Donzoko, four or five of my mates were there to meet us. Everyone was able to speak some English, though not fluently, so Angela was bombarded with questions. The questions were mostly silly and basic, for instance, 'What do you think of Japan?'; 'Do you like the Japanese people?'; 'Do you like Tokyo?'; 'Which is more fun, London or Tokyo?'; 'Who do you prefer, the Beatles or the Rolling Stones?'

Certainly, it is difficult to give *proper* answers to these questions. Every time they asked her a question, Angela gave a nervous, troubled look. She should have answered with clichés or jokes. Instead, with an earnest expression on her face, Angela stammered to reply, 'I can't say for sure, because I've only seen the surface, but I think from what I have experienced so far, Tokyo is a chaotic place where East and West mix. Neither the town itself nor the people in it are orderly. However, Tokyo is a safe town with few crimes, and the underground almost always runs on time. That's really quite incredible.' When one of us said, 'That's the problem with Japan! It's so chaotic and disorderly,' Angela immediately became defensive, 'I didn't say it was bad to be chaotic.'

The night deepened as our conversation stretched into the late hours. My mates seemed very satisfied with this strange newcomer, but Angela was somewhat tense the entire night, and occasionally looked tired and annoyed.

She was ill humoured on the train home and also back at our apartment. While we were drinking tea, she burst out angrily, 'Why do Japanese men ask such uninteresting questions? Do they only have childish things in their heads?' I defended them saying, 'They asked those kinds of questions only because they can't speak English well, and can't handle more complicated issues. Despite their language deficiencies, they tried their best to ask many questions, you see. They must have liked you a lot.' She then recovered from her tantrum a little.

After that day, I took Angela to Shinjuku several times, whenever I met up with my mates. However, the communication between Angela and my mates did not progress one bit. On the contrary, it became more and more tedious. Soon, Angela completely lost interest in my mates, and started speaking ill of them when we were alone together. Her slanders were of a childish nature, though. For instance, 'So-and-so looks like a mouse. I don't like that kind of face'; 'The choice of clothes of so-and-so is terrible'; 'Why is so-and-so always silent? He has nothing to say, I bet'; 'The laughter of so-and-so is too superficial, it gives me the creeps. I don't want to talk to someone who sneers like that.'

After awhile, she refused to meet my mates altogether, saying, 'I don't like to waste my time on boring, meaningless conversation.' I understand why she felt like that. When I was with my mates, we naturally talked in Japanese. Apart from when some of us would speak to Angela in broken English out of charity, Angela was left alone, not comprehending a word of our conversation. This must have been dreadfully boring for someone as talkative as Angela.

Even if someone spoke to her, the conversation rarely became interesting, due to the other person's poor command of English. Angela, who valued conversation that was sincere, intelligent, honest, and mature, could not enjoy childish jokes in broken English, so time spent with my friends seemed to her as nothing but a silly waste. Once a person feels that way, everyone in the group starts to look idiotic with nothing interesting to say.

It might have been all right if everyone just looked idiotic. However, Angela became nervous when she was surrounded by unfamiliar languages or habits. She was one of those people who became anxious when in a culture or language different from their own. To hide her inner anxiety, or perhaps even anger, she pretended to be unnecessarily disinterested. Her disinterest soon turned into contempt, revealed in her looks and words.

Angela's immature attitude became even more obvious when a young Japanese girl was among us. Perhaps she hated Japanese girls, or looked down on them. Maybe it was both. Either way, if there was a Japanese girl in our group, Angela would ignore her as much as possible after greeting her with only a brief 'Hello.' Angela's dislike of young Japanese girls was intense, even though she knew almost nothing about them. Did she hate them because their existence seemed so incomprehensible and alien to her? Or was it because they swiftly stole, in a mysterious way that Angela did not comprehend, men's attentions, which Angela thought should have remained on herself?

To compete with other white women for male attention, especially European male attention, must have been a familiar game for Angela. Even if a woman with big breasts like Marilyn Monroe was sitting nearby, most men with a bit of intelligence would fall for Angela instead, as she casually flaunted her profound knowledge, led the conversation by mixing in her uniquely artistic expressions, and articulated what men really wanted to say by occasionally using vulgar words. Angela must have been quite a master in this game of intelligence and latent eroticism.

However, Angela's conversational technique did not work when a Japanese woman was in the party. Over forty years ago in Japan, almost no young women in Japan employed Angela's technique to attract male attention. Thus, Japanese men did not know how to communicate with a woman like Angela, and did not respond well to such techniques as Angela used. This may be unchanged even today. They instead paid attention to pretty young women behaving childishly – the sheer opposite of Angela. To these men, the definition of an attractive woman was one that behaved cutely and childishly. And to get to know such a woman was a trophy for them.

After awhile, Angela stopped coming to the gatherings with my mates altogether, though she kept an acquaintance with one of them. The one she kept in touch with was a guy who was fluent in Italian and was fairly good at English, too.

Around the same time, I myself came to a conclusion similar to the one Angela made. I had accompanied Angela several times to the gatherings of white people she had befriended in Tokyo at coffee houses or restaurants. I had not enjoyed the time with them, though this was most likely due to my poor English ability. Still, I decided to no longer join Angela at such gatherings.

Incidentally, the white acquaintances of Angela were mostly either British or European, with few American exceptions. There were no black people, Middle Eastern people, or Asians. Whether skin colour somehow dictated this formation of a white-only group on the other side of the world, or if it was the grim reality of racial discrimination, I am not sure. Regardless, Caucasians only socialized with other Caucasians at that time.

On My English Ability

Some readers might think it strange whenever I write, 'due to my poor English ability.' They may even point out the fact that I was able to talk with Angela about literature, politics, religion, or anything, really. Take the first time I met with Angela, for instance. Did I not realize that I was able to intimately communicate with her while talking about politics and so on?

Yes, that is true. But to have a one-on-one conversation about a clearly defined subject matter is totally different from a group chit-chat over a drink. When talking casually with several friends, there usually is not a specific topic to begin with. The conversation may touch on politics, then move onto a sexual matter, then to one person's sexual encounter in childhood, then to another's relationship with their parents, then to yet another's recollection of his elementary school, then suddenly the topic jumps to the shortcomings of the current educational system in Britain... That's the way casual conversation goes. Often, the cue for a topical transition in the course of a conversation can be a small joke.

When it is a one-on-one conversation on a set topic, someone like me who learned English from books and newspapers can handle and enjoy it, to an extent. However, when one joins *ad hoc* chit-chat with several people on no particular topic, one needs a completely different sensibility and set of language abilities in order to be able to enjoy it. For example, in the case of one-on-one conversation, when one has difficulty understanding a word, an expression, or the content, one can ask for a definition each time. On the other hand, in the case of casual chit-chat, it would be too embarrassing to ask each time one comes across something one does not understand, because everyone is there to kill time and be entertained, having no other meaningful or interesting thing to do. They are less inclined to exchange insightful opinions or to obtain some kind of meaningful knowledge.

Forty years ago, twenty-five year old me had neither the language ability nor the conversational skills to deal with casual chatter, nor the maturity to nonchalantly smile if I was left behind in a conversation. Instead, I felt bored and irritated, but pretended to be uninterested. I did not want my inner turmoil to show. So, I would often crack a vulgar joke or two and leave. Before long, I distanced myself from that group of Caucasians much older than myself, who all seemed to enjoy themselves in Tokyo as they pleased (or so it seemed to me). I seldom communicated with them afterwards.

The Typical Lives of Caucasians in Tokyo

Let me describe how Angela and I enjoyed Tokyo. We would leave our apartment in Meguro together and head for Shinjuku. Once in Shinjuku, we arranged when and where to meet again that night and parted ways to have fun with our own friends separately. This odd arrangement for enjoying our evenings worked quite well.

Excluding the fact that Angela lived with me, she otherwise led a typical Tokyo life for a foreigner, or rather, for a Caucasian. She only communicated with other white people living in Tokyo, except when she worked at NHK. She formed her opinions about Japanese culture, politics, and social issues based on the information shared among Caucasians, and acted accordingly. Even when she became acquainted with Japanese people fluent in English, she never saw them in private. There must have been many workers proficient in English at NHK, but she never met up with any of them at restaurants or anywhere else, and never introduced them to me. She rarely talked about them in the first place.

Angela was not very interested in, and sometimes even positively hated, Japanese men over twenty-five years old. Several times, Angela said, 'Until the age of twenty-five, Japanese men are all easy-going, beautiful, and charming. But over that age, they have a unique lack of charm. Perhaps they are victims of the rigidness and oppression of Japanese society.' Whenever I travel abroad and observe Japanese men on foreign street corners, I find myself sharing a similar opinion. Angela's view is therefore understandable. Yet then I must ask, why was she so obsessed with me? It's a mystery. Well, I did happen to be exactly twenty-five years old that year.

Angela once went to see *kabuki*,[3] saying she got a free ticket. The ticket was obtained through one of her British

---

[3] *Kabuki*: classical Japanese theatre known for its stylistic performances and elaborate make-up. Originally, it started in the Edo period as an all-female performance art, but after female performers were banned by the authorities, it transformed into an all-male art, and flourished. Today, some *kabuki* troupes use female actors in female roles, but major theatres still retain the all-male tradition.

acquaintances that I had never met, and she went with a couple of British friends. Before she went, she asked me what I thought of *kabuki*. 'Worthless. It attests to the lack of philosophy in Japanese culture. Well, think of it as an opera,' I said. Angela was pleased to hear my uncouth opinion. After the viewing, she returned with her own opinion, which was rather impressive. 'As you said, *kabuki* has no philosophy at all, and it may indeed be worthless. But it resembles *manga* a lot. It's not too much to say that they are formed from the same sentiment. I feel like I understand Japan a bit more now,' said Angela. To be sure, *manga* and *kabuki* both became very popular in Japan in the following years, and now both are renowned and greatly respected the world over as products of Japanese culture. In a way, Angela more or less foretold the future of Japanese culture.

Phobia of Japanese Women

Angela had a certain opinion toward Japanese women, the opinion typical of a liberated white woman. 'There are no ugly women in Japan. They may not be beautiful, but they are all pretty and charming in their own way.' She often said this, and appeared to feel some attraction toward them. Yet, she never liked them. Deep down, she disparaged and hated them.

What especially got on her nerves was the way Japanese women tried to make themselves look unnecessarily cute and childish, and how they also pretended to be excessively conservative and domestic. Whenever she witnessed such behaviour in Japanese women, she signalled at me with a scornful sneer, and mumbled some untranslatable vulgar words, expressing her disgust. Angela thought Japanese women tried to look prettier and more conservative than they actually were because they had no aspirations to be independent, and wanted men to protect them.

Perhaps the Japanese women at that time had fewer aspirations to be independent, of which Angela was convinced. However, I need to add in defence of Japanese women that their coquettish behaviour was actually not as simple as Angela thought. Allow me to explain. Today, we have many successful businesswomen, company executives, and professionals, such as medical doctors and lawyers, among Japanese women. If Angela's (rather popular) theory were true, these successful women would have stopped trying to look overly young and cute. However, to my own surprise, once they are out of the office and are in a wine bar or *karaoke* bar, these successful women try to look even younger and prettier than typical female office workers do.

In my opinion, to look naïve and pretty has nothing to do with independence, success, or liberation in Japan. It is a deep-seated and peculiar aesthetic value and sensibility in the heart of Japanese women. You may call it cultural DNA, for instance, just as Japanese men in their fifties with executive status want to flick through *manga* from time to time.

Another thing peculiar to Japanese women is that they do not hesitate to marry men of any race or nationality. If they feel like it, they date African, Middle Eastern, Chinese, Korean, and, of course, Caucasian men and marry them.

Japanese men, on the other hand, can do nothing but live 'conservatively.' They live restricted lives no matter where they are. They criticize Japanese women's behaviour, slandering them by saying, 'Japanese women are not chaste. White women would never marry black men,' grotesquely praising white women. In my opinion, Japanese women are far from conservative; in fact, they are totally uninhibited.

Chapter 4

Second-Rate Films at Second-Rate Cinemas

Angela looked happy as long as she was with me, as I wrote previously. When we talked, whatever I said – even if it was foolish – seemed to sound exquisite to her. Spurred by my 'exquisite' utterance, she herself would become talkative. Even when I started a silly argument, she would turn it into a stimulating, enjoyable, and interesting discussion.

When we had nothing to talk about, we spent time quietly reading books. While reading books, often we suddenly broke into a conversation on what we had just encountered in the reading, sometimes criticizing or finding fault with, and sometimes praising, what we had just read. We also frequently went to the cinema together. I learned a lot from Angela about European existentialist films, which I had found difficult to understand until that point. For instance, I grasped for the first time Michelangelo Antonioni's intention in making his films and what messages the films carried. Until then, they had seemed nothing but a bore to me.

We watched many Japanese films, too. The films we saw at cheap cinemas were nothing like the artsy ones that received awards at European film festivals, but rather tawdry ones featuring mafia, detectives, or love stories. When I thought certain lines needed to be translated for Angela in order for her to follow the storyline, I whispered the translation to Angela. Sometimes Angela asked for my translation by whispering in my ear. I hope we did not bother the audience too much….

Angela spoke highly of Japanese actors in the films, male or female, saying 'very beautiful, very sexy.' She was profoundly fascinated by the men and women in *yakuza* films, and praised them using the word, 'super.' When a tattooed back of a *yakuza* male was shown, she held her breath and stared at it. She also liked sword swingers that featured Na-

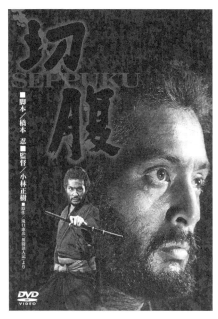

Nakadai Tatsuya on the cover of DVD

kadai Tatsuya.[1] To a white woman's eyes, he looked beautiful and sexy.

Yuzo Kayama,[2] on the other hand, stirred no interest in Angela as he was, in her words, 'not at all sexy.' She called Koji Ishizaka[3] 'beautiful' and admitted he was handsome, but said he was 'neither sexy, nor attractive.' She called every leading Japanese actress 'pretty,' 'cute,' and 'beautiful.'

Yuzo Kayama on the cover of his record.

Angela found second-rate Japanese entertainment films, including the 'Nikkatsu Roman Porno' series,[4] generally entic-

---

[1] Tatsuya Nakadai is a Japanese actor born in 1932. He is praised for his immaculate acting and has been favoured by big names in the Japanese film industry, such as Kon Ichikawa, Akira Kurosawa, Hiroshi Teshigawara, and Kihachi Okamoto.

[2] Yuzo Kayama is also a Japanese actor, born in 1937. He was especially popular in the sixties for his role in a film series called 'Wakadaisho (The Young Ace).'

[3] Koji Ishizaka is another Japanese actor, born in 1941. He has been more active on TV than in the film industry.

ing. She was very curious about the morality and aestheticism peculiar to Japanese people exhibited in these unsophisticated, vulgar films. The less artistic the film was, the less European or American influence she thought she found in it, and the more raw culture unique to Japan she could discover.

Angela's passion worked both for and against her purpose. The more B-movies she watched, the more she came to realize that the Japanese morality and philosophy at the spiritual core of these films were essentially the same as in Christianity. For instance, Angela used to think virginity and chastity were not important in Japanese culture, and that Japanese people enjoyed sex more freely and uninhibitedly. (In my opinion, her idea was probably affected by pornographic colour prints produced in the Edo era, such as the ones by Utamaro, which were popular among Europeans. She might also have been influenced by her readings about the Japanese tradition of '*yobai.*'[5]) However, after watching many second-rate Japanese films, it dawned on her that Japanese people were even more repressed with regard to sexuality than European Christians. After that, Japanese people appeared to her as less free and less liberated in their daily lives. Angela was disappointed

---

[4] Nikkatsu Roman Porno: Hundreds of pornographic films produced by Japanese film company Nikkatsu between 1971-1988. Nikkatsu was a major film company in the sixties, and created countless great films, but slowly declined as the number of viewers fell. Nikkatsu concentrated on producing low-budget pornographic films to save the company, which temporarily succeeded as the Roman Porno series gained a huge audience. However, when mass-produced porn videos came into fashion, Nikkatsu stopped their production.

to realize that the Japanese and Europeans were not that different. Japanese popular culture, which had once piqued her curiosity, suddenly lost its allure. Angela stopped watching second-rate Japanese films.

Contrary to her long-held belief, what she learned was that the Judeo-Christian culture was not so unique, after all. Its morality, its view of the world, and its philosophy, she realized, could be found on the other side of the world, held by people belonging to a culture that had nothing to do with Judaism or Christianity. More disappointingly, she came to realize that Europeans polluted by Judeo-Christianity were not the only people that were repressed. She learned that, even in remote Japan, people – including *yakuza* men, prostitutes, female teachers, and male students in love with female teachers – were all living 'unliberated' lives, bound by a morality and philosophy similar to Christianity-contaminated Europeans.

Poor Angela – she gradually grew unable to enjoy the victim mentality and elitism typical of the European intelligentsia. In fact, I gradually heard her utter the term 'Judeo-Christian culture' less and less as time passed.

---

[5] '*Yobai*' literally means 'night-time crawling.' Historically, it was a custom widely practiced in Japan in which a man snuck into a woman's room to have sex. The marriage practice in pre-modern Japan was partly considered '*yobai*' as well, as a wife would continue to live in her parents' house while her husband would pay her visits. However, at present '*yobai*' is generally a term used for unmarried couples.

Fireworks

We once went to see fireworks together on a riverbank in the suburbs of Tokyo.[6] I do not remember the details of this short trip, except that it was very boring. To us Japanese, a fireworks festival on some riverbank is a mundane, ordinary event repeated since childhood, thus the thought of going to another one brought no excitement whatsoever to the twenty-five year old me.

After exiting a suburban train station, we were jostled forward by the crowd. We walked along the riverbank, squashed by the crowd, looking up from time to time to watch fiery balls of red, blue, and yellow spread across the night sky. I found the fireworks, which we call '*hanabi,*' not at all interesting because I had seen them so many times since I was a kid. The meaninglessness of it, my boredom, and the noisy crowd merely irritated me. Come to think of it, festivals held throughout the year at Japanese shrines and temples are also generally silly, boring, noisy, and crowded. I remember feeling terribly edgy that night when I went to watch the fireworks with Angela. Irritated, I longed for the noise and the crowds of Shinjuku. Was the crowd at the fireworks festival any different from the crowds in Shinjuku? To me, they seemed totally opposite. Fireworks festivals were domestic events for families, whereas the Shinjuku streets were for unattached

---

[6] According to Gordon, it was 30 July, 1970, that Sozo and Angela went to see a fireworks display (p. 166).

young men and women to meet one another, away from their families.

A Kind-hearted White Woman

It is generally said in Japan that Japanese women are kind-hearted and generous to men, whereas white women are harsh and cold-hearted. I wonder if that holds any truth. When I was living with Angela, I never thought of her as cold-hearted or harsh, not even once. Far from being harsh, she was almost always very generous and kind. Gentle sparkles were nearly always in her eyes. When we were having a cup of coffee at a café, or sitting on a bench in a park, she would survey her surroundings quietly, her eyes filled with kindness. It was not a cold stare that rejected the people and things around her; her gaze was one that tried to understand, forgive, and embrace as much as possible, come what may.

Even now, I can vividly picture in my mind her gentle, calm, violet eyes as she casually surveyed her surroundings at a café or park. More than anything, I liked her generous gaze and face on such occasions.

Often, when Angela was in a good mood or feeling energetic, or on mornings when she felt happy, she would prepare a cup of tea, pancakes, and slices of apple for me and bring them to me when I was still half-asleep in bed. Japanese mothers and wives traditionally do not do such a thing, so I was intrigued. Angela would say something like, 'Darling, wake up,' and eye me kindly. I remember how happy it made me, feeling her deep love. The actual eating and drinking in bed in a not fully awake state did not suit me though, because it made my stomach bloated. Eventually, after perhaps getting bored with offering such English-style services, she stopped bringing breakfast to me in bed, and started to help herself to toast and a cup of tea at the table. It fit me better. For me, breakfast should be taken at the table, while fully awake.

Happy Times

Angela took time in preparing elaborate breakfasts: making pancakes, cooking omelets, adding salad and fruit on the side, and brewing tea. In comparison, she did not care much about lunch or dinner. As for lunch and dinner, I cooked more than she did. I cooked rice, *miso* soup, and a choice of meat, fish, or vegetables, stir-fried or stewed. I often cooked curry or stew. Sometimes I made *sukiyaki*, or even *tempura*.

Angela enjoyed eating whatever I cooked, but she especially liked *tempura*, calling it 'super.' For some reason, I have been good at cooking *tempura* ever since I was a child. When I was a student, I cooked *tempura* at a friend's place, and he said to me, 'You'd better quit writing bad novels and open a *tempura* restaurant instead.'

Angela not only enjoyed the food I prepared for her, she also enjoyed traditional Japanese food (the English are well-known for not being fastidious about food – it may be true, but it is not necessarily a bad thing. They are happy to eat whatever is offered to them without complaining, just as the Japanese do). Angela particularly liked *tofu*. She would heat it in a ceramic pot, and eat it with a spoon, sprinkling a bit of soy sauce on top. She even liked a bowl of wholegrain rice with *tsukudani*,[7] though she could not stomach *natto*.[8]

It made me feel content to see her sitting directly on *tatami* mats and happily eating simple meals such as that. While eating those humble meals, she loved talking about Basho Matsuo or Issa Kobayashi. Her generosity and intelligence on such occasions touched me in a very deep part of my soul. I now think this image of Angela fits my idea of the perfect woman. Talking with Angela about Japanese literature, going back as far as *The Tale of Genji*, surely resembled what I vaguely pictured in my mind as romantic bliss.

Whether it was in our small apartment in Tokyo, or in a huge room with twenty *tatami* mats in an oceanfront villa in Kujukuri, looking out onto the Pacific Ocean, the most enjoyable and memorable moments to me were those meal times, when we talked about literature and philosophy, scooping up *tofu* from a ceramic pot together. I learned, however, the best moments to Angela were different from the ones I would have chosen. I still remember it after forty years: we were sitting in the sun at the villa in Kujukuri, sipping Japanese tea, and talking about Faulkner, I believe. I said to Angela, 'If we eventually separate and look back on our time together, I'm sure I'll recall the conversations we had, like this one, as our best moments. The conversations we had on literature and so

---

[7] *Tsukudani*: either small fish, shellfish, or seaweed that has been prepared by boiling it down with soy sauce and sugar, to eat with rice.

[8] *Natto*: fermented soy beans.

on.' Then Angela said something quite surprising, 'To me, the best moments with you that would stick out in my mind are nothing like that. They're more sexual, and go like this: in the morning, after having sex, both of us are content, and lying in bed half-asleep, and I feel the warmth of your body. Those moments – a little tired, but peaceful and content – are the best. I'll never forget those erotic moments, filled with the scent of your body and the sound of your breathing.' That is what Angela said.

At the time, when I heard that, I thought Angela and I had totally different concepts of romantic bliss. I took it as a gender difference, rather than as a personal difference between Angela and me. (To prevent misunderstanding, I would like, perhaps unnecessarily, to add that at the time I did not think of the difference as a cultural one between the Japanese and the British.)

But now that I look back forty years later, it dawns on me that our two views might have been similar, after all, though expressed differently. It seems to me we had more or less the same image of ultimate happiness in our minds, only we described it from two different angles.

To add some more about our eating habits, I cooked more often than Angela did while we lived together. I did the cooking and Angela did the washing and cleaning up. She became fed up with washing dishes, and often complained, saying, 'Let me do something more creative.' She could not cook well, however, so I continued cooking, and she had to endure doing the more tedious chores.

Walking

Both Angela and I loved to walk. Perhaps Angela did not like it as much as I did, but agreed to walk with me only because I liked it so much. Either way, we walked a lot together.

We walked endlessly in the parks of Tokyo, in the affluent residential area near Meguro, and to a town further down with many cheap apartments – a reminder of the nationwide poverty just after the war – and through an anachronistic shopping arcade adjacent to it, and so on and so on. As we walked, we always chatted. The topic could be the *buraku*[9] people in Japan, or Shakespeare, or Marquis de Sade, or Sartre and Existentialism, or even classical Japanese art forms, such as the tea ceremony or flower arrangement.

Angela was especially amused when I did not think highly of Edo culture, such as the tea ceremony, flower arrangement, *haiku*, and *kabuki*. In my opinion, those stupid arts established themselves by paying too much attention to pointless details and inventing foolishly complicated rules. They paralleled Japan's refusal to develop outwardly as it isolated itself within international society and turned inward instead.[10] She laughed

---

[9] *Buraku*: originally, the word only meant 'a village,' but historically, it came to mean the segregated villages for the people traditionally discriminated against, from the lowest class of the pre-modern system. The movement for *buraku* equality has been ongoing since the Meiji period, and continues today.

[10] The author refers to the policy of national isolation, the banning of international communication and trade, taken by the Tokugawa government during the Edo era, from 1639 to 1854.

delightedly every time I voiced such an opinion. It seems the contrast between me and the other highly educated people in Japan she met at NHK or other places was interesting to her. As soon as they met Angela, most Japanese were happy to talk about the artistry of Edo culture, like flower arrangement, the tea ceremony, or *kabuki*.

One of the topics we talked about frequently was the Profumo Affair. Having read several books on the affair around that time, I had become fascinated by the key person, a prostitute named Christine Keeler. She had been sleeping with John Profumo, Secretary of State for War, as well as Dr. Stephen Ward, an osteopath, who was rumoured to be her stage manager. So, quite one-sidedly, I talked about it to Angela and shot questions at her.

I once said naïvely, 'I heard Profumo wrote love letters to Christine Keeler. So he had some amount of affection for her, I assume?' Angela retorted with a coolness unusual to her, 'He might have written, "I love you" on an office notepad, but don't you realize it had nothing to do with love? You'd better grow up, darling.' Incidentally, I do not particularly dislike that kind of hypocritical behaviour between Western men and women.

We did not just chat when we walked; sometimes, we actually sang songs by Elvis or The Beatles. Angela's voice was quite deep when speaking, but when she sang, it rose in pitch. It was a crystal-clear voice, particular to Scandinavian white women. (I do not suppose many people except myself have heard Angela Carter sing. Not many people in England sing in public, and Angela did not sing either at first whenever I sang. But gradually, she began singing as if she could not help but join me, because I seemed to have so much fun.)

As for music, Angela professed to like Bob Dylan. But, I think the singer she liked best was a German baritone, Dietrich Fischer-Dieskau. She repeatedly praised him with fervour, saying, 'When I hear him sing, I'm moved to tears.'

When we got tired of walking, we would drop by a café on a street corner and have a cup of coffee. She always added some water to the coffee. 'Japanese coffee is too strong and too hot,' she used to say.

In those days, there were many unique cafés with individual interiors, decorations, and music that reflected their owners' tastes and principles. Angela liked to visit various cafés to find the uniqueness of each one. I wonder what she would have said if she looked at today's standardized coffee shops, not only in Tokyo, but all over Japan. She certainly would have been very disappointed.

The season changed from spring to summer, and when summer (which was 'as crazy as the Japanese people,' as Angela described) was at its end, Angela began to surface out of the foreigners-only community in which she had been taking refuge. She sometimes came to a disco and danced with my friends or friends of friends, or talked with them until morning at a jazz café. Not infrequently, that nervous and anxious look of hers would reappear on her face, but compared to a few months earlier, she was far more relaxed and able to communicate with Japanese people more easily. She had probably got used to the broken, imperfect English spoken by the Japanese. She also probably learned the deeper meaning hidden behind the childish expressions used by the Japanese, because she was no longer alarmed by the overly simplistic and superficial language and expressions the Japanese tended to employ when speaking English, due to their poor English ability.

From time to time, a thirty-something British man, John, who called himself an Oxford graduate, joined our group. He was said to be fluent in Japanese, but I rarely heard him speak either in Japanese or English. He was a quiet man. One day, he brought a booklet written in Japanese and showed me an article in it. As I read it, he said, 'I wrote that piece.' It was written in perfect, error-free Japanese from beginning to end. I became suspicious for a moment, thinking, 'Can a foreigner write such perfect Japanese, even if he is quite good at it?' I complimented it anyway, saying, 'Oh, wonderful, really great.' Strangely, a few days later, I heard from Angela that John had confessed to her that he had not written the article after all, and that he had asked her not to tell me. I thought then, 'What a strange lie he told. He may be an honest guy after all, since he confessed.' Thinking of him again, his being an Oxford graduate also sounds suspicious. If he was not truthful about a small article, he may very well have been lying about Oxford, too. Then again, he did not confess to Angela that his *alma mater* was a lie. So was it true? I wonder where that quiet British liar is now, and what he is doing.

Professionalism

While we were living together, I witnessed the very professional writer in Angela on several occasions. She was not just a bookish girl, all grown up. Once, we met a friend of mine from university, who was about to go to the U.S. to study advertising. He had his own theory of dividing cultures into two groups, the hard and the soft, to draw some kind of conclusion (though what conclusion, I do not recall), and he explained his theory to us. I was rather pleased to see my friend speaking in English about his own theory, whatever it may have been.

Angela listened intently at first, but after a while, she began to criticize him in a ridiculing tone, 'According to your theory, Dostoyevsky is soft, Tolstoy is hard, Hemingway is hard, Scott Fitzgerald is soft, Tanizaki is soft, Soseki is hard, right?' She continued listing names, as if she were telling some kind of a joke.

Detecting a mocking tone in Angela's voice, a perplexed and embarrassed look appeared on my friend's face. 'Don't you think it's a bit too simplistic of an idea that even a high school student who's fond of books could come up with? What's the point in writing an article based on it?' Angela's criticism was merciless. She went on rather jokingly, 'Culture is not so simple that it can be divided into hard and soft, is it? Is what you're doing any different from what a clerk selling vacuum cleaners does, telling customers there are two kinds of vacuum cleaners?'

At that time, my friend was writing up an English version

of his theory under the guidance of some American tutor. Apparently no one, including his tutor, had ever ridiculed his theory before Angela. He must have expected Angela to praise his theory, to say 'good idea' or at least something similar, but Angela's reaction was the exact opposite. He tried hard to smile, but his face was frozen in his bewilderment.

What struck me most then was not what Angela said, but how she said it: the way she ridiculed him with her tone of voice, facial expression, and body language. When someone said something disagreeable regarding her own profession or what mattered to her, she was ready to attack him or her as sadistically as possible. I found that interesting. Amateurs like me pretend to agree with others, no matter what they say, and smile away the awkwardness by saying, 'Well, well, that is interesting, isn't it?' Angela showed me the severity and intensity of a professional writer with regard to a matter I thought to be minor.

On another occasion, on a hot day in August, another friend of mine from university visited our flat in Meguro in order to commission a PR job from Angela; he wanted Angela to write a small piece of advertising. Angela agreed to do it, on the condition that she used a pseudonym. While we talked about this job, she was the usual Angela Carter: carefree, frank, and a little sarcastic, as I'd seen at cafés and bars in Shinjuku. Later, we paid a visit to the advertising company my friend worked for. I went along as her interpreter, since the person in charge could not speak English. Angela drastically transformed when she met the person in charge at the office. In an instant, Angela turned into a different person: one who was very serious, courteous, and friendly, without a shred of sarcasm or carefree frankness.

I was greatly impressed at seeing Angela transform within seconds when it came to her job. 'She really does earn her living with a pen,' I marvelled. Looking back, however, I suspect she changed into a different person not only because of her job. Angela might have sensed, as soon as she saw the person in charge, that she would not get along with him – that he was not her type. She then perhaps decided not to expose her true self to a person she would not like much, but instead to dutifully perform her social role as a professional writer. This was not the only occasion on which she acted this way. She always followed her womanly intuition, decisively choosing what role to play.

Blueprint for a Love Tragedy

As I wrote before, I never felt Angela was in any way opposite from, or alien to, me. Rather, I felt as if she had been right next to me since I was a child, as if she had been someone very familiar with whom I had always kept close contact – a childhood playmate, for instance, on whom I could rely in good times or bad. Perhaps, as a girlfriend, she might have been too familiar or too similar to me. I was able to understand her most of the time, though there were times when I could not, due to my poor English. She had a peculiar sensibility, but it was not unpleasant to me.

I am sure, at least while we were together, she felt the same way as I did. Once we even talked, half-jokingly, about a plan to co-author a novel. It was about a single Japanese man and a married British woman a bit older than him. They meet in New York, fall in love, live together in Tokyo for a while, and start thinking about marriage. However, they have many obstacles, such as cultural differences between Japan and the UK, racial discrimination they encounter, their own problems with their families and friends, her existing marriage, and her age. In the end, they give up on the idea of marriage and separate, though they are still very much in love. Needless to say, the novel did not materialize.

Angela and I never really discussed getting married. A few months into our cohabitation, Angela said, 'Marriage is not much different from this. It is boring, isn't it?' After that, neither of us mentioned marriage. I do not know what was truly in Angela's mind, but I myself had never thought of marrying her.

Now, I wonder why the idea of marriage never occurred to us. After all, we were an adult heterosexual couple living together. At the time, I had never pictured marriage as a realistic option, and did not particularly think about marrying Angela. What was in Angela's mind, I wonder? She used to say the kind of thing a progressive woman in those days would: 'Marriage itself is an old institution; it has lost its significance in modern society.' But, how did she feel about it in truth? She had been married for ten years, though she was separated from her husband by that time. When I asked why she got married in the first place, she said, 'When he proposed to me,

I thought that it might be the last chance for me to get married. So I accepted his proposal.' When I said, 'That's contradictory to what you're always advocating, isn't it?' she retorted, 'Have I ever said that I have no contradictions? I am a contradictory woman.' A contradictory woman? Well, she was one for sure. I never knew how to react to that 'so-what' attitude.

The Country Villa at Kujukuri

The stifling hot and humid summer was over. That summer had been unbearable even to the Japanese, and, according to Angela, it made her wonder why the Japanese did not go mad and start killing one another. The autumnal breeze blew in, signalling that winter was close at hand. It was at about the end of November, I believe, when we vacated our apartment in Meguro and moved into a villa in Kujukuri.[11]

Kujukuri Beach is a seaside town facing the Pacific Ocean, about a hundred kilometres east of Tokyo. The beach received its name from the fact that it stretched over forty kilometres. (Kujukuri literally means the Japanese equivalent of 400 kilometres. The actual beach is not as long as that, though. The name exaggerates its length.)

The villa we moved into retained its original Japanese farmland cottage appearance (with a thatched roof, if I remember correctly) and part of its interior, divided by *fusuma*[12] into three *tatami* rooms. But the area that used to be a

---

[11] According to Gordon, it was 29 November, 1970. Four days before their departure to Kujukuri, Mishima committed suicide (p. 171).

doma[13] was renovated and covered with wooden flooring, and equipped with a fireplace.

The villas nearby were frequently used by foreigners. The house next to the one we moved into was owned by Edward Seidensticker, a famous scholar of Japanese literature. Yukio Mishima, as well as Donald Keene, were rumoured to have been spotted there a few times.

If my memory is correct, we left the apartment in Meguro, spent a night at 'honest' John's place, and moved to Kujukuri in his car the next day. We entered the house from the *doma* into a *tatami* room, and found a harpsichord sitting at the end of it. Between the front of the villa and the beach along the Pacific was a pine tree grove. This grove stretched all the way along the beach, and a number of two-storied, Western-style villas were located in the grove. (When you think of the *tsunami* triggered by the earthquake in March 2011, our villa was in a terrible location.)

If you went through the woods heading inland, a sandy path (which somehow reminded me of *Woman in the Dunes* by Kobo Abe) ran parallel to both the grove and the beach,

---

[12] *Fusuma:* rectangular panels used to divide a room in Japanese architecture. They slide from side to side and can function as doors. They usually have a wooden understructure covered with layers of paper on both sides.

[13] *Doma:* an area in a traditional Japanese house located between the living quarters and the outside. This area is used as a kitchen or a working space, and the floor is covered with dirt, usually at the same level as the outside road surface. The living quarter, on the other hand, is lifted one level up, and you need to take off your shoes to go out of the *doma* and into the living quarters. In modern houses, a *doma* remains only as an entrance area, where you take off your shoes.

and beyond the path were rice paddies interspersed with some farmhouses.

The Pacific was to the exact east of our villa. When we woke up early in the morning, or when we stayed up all night talking, we often saw the sun rise straight up from the endlessly vast, wide ocean. On a particularly sunny morning, all of the fishermen's families gathered together to pull a dragnet up onto the beach. It had been brought to the beachside by a fishing boat, which was moored at the beachhead. Seeing several fishermen's families all gathered on the beach like that, vivid scenes from my childhood of rice planting and harvesting came back to me. They were peaceful memories of the countryside, in stark contrast to life in Tokyo, especially Shinjuku.

In the *tatami* room of this seaside house, sitting on a cushion placed on *tatami* mats and facing a typewriter on a coffee table, Angela began writing a novel, which was published later under the title *Love*.[14] I also began writing a story. The story went like this: A small, out-of-the-way seaside village is panic-stricken when a few village girls and married women are seduced by a handsome serial killer and are murdered

---

[14] His memory here might not be correct. It was *The Infernal Desire Machines of Doctor Hoffman* that Carter wrote in Kujukuri, according to Susan Rubin Sleiman. She writes that Carter told her that 'she wrote the novel in three months, in a Japanese fishing village on an island.' See 'The Fate of the Surrealist Imagination' in Lorna Sage, ed., *Flesh and the Mirror: Essays on the Art of Angela Carter*, Virago, 1994, pp.98-116 (p.110). Sleiman's comment is verified by Carter's journal entry (see Afterword).

afterwards in a sickening way. The main plot is narrated to the reader through the conversations between a young English teacher and a middle-aged woman; the former has come to the village as a private tutor and the latter becomes his lover. At the end, this middle-aged woman voluntarily falls prey to the handsome killer and is killed by him. When I told this unimaginative and unrealistic story to Angela, she asked, 'What is that handsome serial killer anyway?' When I told her, 'He is a symbolic male that brings change to outmoded Japanese society, like Nietzsche's Superman,'[15] she slandered it in two words: 'Too stupid.' 'The most boring story is one about a Superman.' Though I saw her point, I continued writing it, because I still found the story interesting. When I penned about half of it, however, I stopped – not because its theme and storyline ceased to engage me, but because I realized my descriptive skill was too feeble to make this unrealistic story sound real. I came to the conclusion that I should perhaps write nonfiction, about what really exists around me, on the topics I know. (When I told a friend how I changed my mind about writing novels, he said, 'Did you really have such a stupid epiphany? The topics you're familiar with can't possibly offer enough interesting material to write about!' His opinion also rings true, I think.)

---

[15] Superman: originally Übermensche, a concept in the philosophy of Friedrich Nietzsche, described as a goal for humanity in *Thus Spoke Zarathustra*, published in 1883. It was translated by Thomas Common in 1909 as 'Superman,' though the word is criticized today as not correctly capturing the concept.

After I quit writing, I later became interested in the idealism of George Berkeley, the writing method of William Faulkner, and the surrealism of Marquis de Sade, and started to read about them. When I said to Angela one day, 'It would be fun to study philosophy or literature my whole life in a countryside house like this,' she replied, 'That's everyone's dream. But you need money to support such a life. Where would it come from, huh?' That was one hell of a realistic comment – unusual for her.

Chapter 5

Yukio Mishima's Suicide by *Seppuku*[1]

Like two recluses, we lived by the Pacific Ocean in a seaside cottage in Kujukuri between 1970 and 1971. Japan was still caught up in political turbulence. To the disappointment of the left-wingers, the second wave of the so-called *Anpo* Strife[2] ended without inciting any major movement. Another group of youths with an extreme leftist ideology had appeared on the scene – far more radical and militant than those involved in *Anpo*. They had just started a series of terrorist attacks.

In such a political climate, Yukio Mishima shocked society with his suicide by *seppuku*. In the morning of 29 November 1970, four men clad in military uniform sneaked into the Ichigaya headquarters of the Japanese Self-Defence Force (SDF) and took a few senior officers hostage. Led by Yukio Mishima, they called themselves members of the *Tate-no-Kai*,[3]

---

[1] *Seppuku*: another way of saying *hara-kiri* (disembowelment).
[2] *Anpo* Strife: a political movement by anti-government and anti-American protestors, opposing the Treaty of Mutual Cooperation and Security between the United States and Japan in 1960. The movement became violent, involving students, workers, and general citizens. The first movement was from 1959 to 1960. The second wave was in 1970.

whose activity until then was virtually unknown to anyone. They demanded all the executive officers of the SDF be summoned to the courtyard. When the officers gathered, Mishima made a speech urging them to join his coup d'état in order to achieve constitutional reform. Contrary to his expectation, however, Mishima failed to persuade the SDF officers to rise up in response to his beautiful and gallant

Yukio Mishima just before *seppuku*.[4]

---

[3] *Tate-no-Kai* translates to Association of the Shield.
[4] Photo reproduced by courtesy of Jiji Press.

speech. He then confined himself in a room, where he stabbed himself in the belly with a Japanese sword he had brought with him, and had his head cut off by a young man named Morita. Morita then committed *seppuku*, and had his head cut off by another youth.

This incident shook Japanese society. It affected the heart of the Japanese people, not only because it was the suicide of a famous author – which was of course significant – but because it was a suicide by *hara-kiri*. It is bewildering when I think that, while we were extremely shaken by this act of *hara-kiri*, we, the Japanese people, did not think deeply about the background of the incident. There was no serious questioning as to why Mishima and his men broke into the headquarters of the SDF, or why Mishima urged the officers to rise up, or what it meant to rise up and what it was for. We knew almost nothing about the *Tate-no-Kai*, nor did we have any interest. I remember reading an article published shortly before the incident. According to the article, the then Director General of the Defence Agency, Mr. Nakasone, a rather insolent man, replied as follows when asked about the '*Tate-no-Kai*': 'It is more similar to the Takarazuka Revue[5] (a musical theatre group

---

[5] The Takarazuka Revue is a Japanese all-female musical theatre founded by Ichizo Kobayashi, a politician and the president of Hankyu Railways. The theatre is based in Takarazuka in Hyogo prefecture. Though it has its enthusiasts, the Takarazuka Revue tends to be considered lower in its artistry than *kabuki*. Nakasone's comment is discriminatory in many ways (sexist, as well as homophobic), as it likens the '*Tate-no-Kai*' to a musical troupe, thus slandering its political ideology, and to an all-female troupe, that is, denying the members' masculinity.

consisting solely of young women) than a militant group with a political ideology.' I remember reading this article with a smirk.

What shook our hearts and stirred our blood, therefore, was nothing more than the *act* of self-disembowelment as a means to die – what Mishima did. It was centuries ago that *seppuku* was acknowledged as an honourable and respected way for *samurai* to put an end to their own lives in the face of dishonour. To our amazement, it was resurrected in the late twentieth century, like an apparition, and was carried out in a brutal, but orderly, manner. It was unlike the cheap, half-baked versions attempted so often by some anachronistic right-wingers, in which they could not kill themselves but instead were rushed to hospitals, where their lives were saved. Mishima's was not at all like theirs. It was an authentic *hara-kiri*, complete with an assistant to chop off his head after Mishima cut his belly open with a Japanese sword.

Not only right-wingers, but also many leftist students, supposedly with oppositional political views, were moved by Mishima's strange performance and praised his act. Assuming a leftist attitude was fashionable at that time in Shinjuku, so it may not have been that surprising that the people claiming to be leftist were touched by Mishima's anachronistic action. I even witnessed a committed left-wing woman, a devoted activist in a labour union, admire Mishima, saying, 'Yukio Mishima did something great.' I also heard a successful, down-to-earth businessman say, 'It was certainly anachronistic, but I don't think I could do the same thing even if I was told to. It was one hell of a courageous act.'

I said to Angela, 'Yukio Mishima had a weak constitution and had to stay at home and read books during his childhood. He didn't play *chambara*[6] like other children. Now, as an adult, he played *chambara* for the first time. Not having developed a proper immunity, he was taken in by the game so much that he ended up forming the *Tate-no-Kai*, which was nothing but an extension of *chambara* play. And he went so far as to perform *hara-kiri* himself.' I also added, 'What he did requires courage, for sure. If living a long life does not automatically guarantee a good life, to die like Mishima might be one possibility, though it is not for everyone.'

Angela did not understand my sentiment, nor did she understand the admiration many Japanese people felt for Mishima. I suppose, seeing the reaction right after Mishima's suicide, she must have felt the Japanese people were crazy and incomprehensible. I remember she wrote an article on the Mishima incident for a British newspaper, in which she wrote, 'My friend S said, "you Westerners will never understand our Japanese mind, because you don't have that kind of passion."'[7]

---

[6] *Chambara*: sword-fighting with fake swords. The term is used for the children's game, as well as for the genre of cinema or television programs based on *samurai* and sword-fighting.

[7] Because the author wrote from his memory, this is not what Angela Carter actually wrote in 'Mishima's Toy Sword,' an article that appeared in *New Society*, in 1971. It reads: "'But,' said my friend, S, 'a European could never understand a thing like Mishima did, because Europeans haven't any passion" (Angela Carter, *Shaking a Leg: Collected Writings*, Penguin Books, 1998 (1997), p.241).

I do not recall telling Angela, 'The Japanese have the kind of passion that you don't.' Moreover, it is unlikely that I would say such a thing. Perhaps she remembered incorrectly, or perhaps, because of our unequal command of English, she misunderstood what I said in my meagre English.

During this talk, I remember that I said something I am still secretly proud of. The topic was on the Japanese people and suicide, especially *hara-kiri*. I said, 'After Emperor Showa made the famous speech accepting our defeat on 15 August 1945, he should have committed suicide by *hara-kiri*. Then he wouldn't have had to disgrace himself by bowing to Douglas McArthur. His humiliating attitude in front of McArthur broke the hearts and crushed the pride of the Japanese people. More than the defeat itself, the undignified image of the Emperor was what made the Japanese spineless in the years afterwards. If the Emperor had committed suicide by *hara-kiri*, the Japanese would have looked at our flag with pride, and sung our national anthem with honour.' Angela, however, showed almost no reaction to this splendid oration of mine.

Seaside Paradise

In those days, political crises were exploding here and there all over the world. Angela and I, however, oblivious to the noise of the world, spent time alone by ourselves at our seaside paradise from late autumn that year to spring the next year, writing, typing, reading, walking, and talking about literature and philosophy.

Some of you may wonder whether we did not get bored

with country life, having lived in busy Tokyo, especially in chaotic Shinjuku. To be sure, for the first week or two, life without a café that offered a good cup of coffee, or a bar for nightly visits, or a *pachinko* place, or a *soba*[8] restaurant, or even a cheap eatery, seemed terribly boring. After a while, though, we got used to it, and this life of nothingness felt incredibly cosy. I talked only with Angela. We cooked and ate together, did what we had to do separately, and went to bed after midnight. I came to have no complaints, and found nothing lacking in such a life. As far as I can remember, I was never irritable being alone with Angela. Moreover, I was never dissatisfied with Angela, nor did I become angry at her during our time by the seaside.

In Tokyo, every little thing had made me edgy, and we argued over trifles, sometimes to the extent that we shouted at each other. During the five months at that spacious cottage on Kujukuri beach, however, Angela and I were kind and gentle with each other, and spent a lovely time together.

Of course, we often visited Tokyo to do some errands. At the beginning, missing the nightlife in Shinjuku, I went to Donzoko for a drink, then to an all-night jazz café in Kabuki-cho with mates and talked some more while sipping cocktails. In the morning, we would move to a tea room to have a cup of coffee, toast and eggs, and talk still more. I would then return to Kujukuri on the morning train. Around the time we greeted the New Year, however, the nightlife in Shinjuku be-

---

[8] *Soba*: Japanese buckwheat noodles.

came unimportant to me. Angela and I would go to Tokyo to run errands, and when they were done, we would say, 'Let's go home,' and we would go straight back to Kujukuri, without seeing anyone or dropping by a bar. Only after a month or so, the cottage in Kujukuri, with its beach and village that had nothing in it, had become 'home' for Angela and me.

Kujukuri Seaside today

During the winter we spent in Kujukuri, the biggest event in Tokyo was *Elvis on Stage* (its original English title was *Elvis: That's the Way It Is*).[9] I went to Yuraku-cho[10] to see it

---

[9] *Elvis: That's the Way It Is*: a documentary film that recorded the stage performances and rehearsals of Elvis Presley. Produced in 1970.

[10] Yuraku-cho: an uptown area next to Ginza. It has many theatres and concert halls.

with Angela. I had been a huge fan of Elvis since my childhood, and excitedly watched his stage performance recorded in the documentary film, the first about Elvis.

Angela saw Elvis sing and dance for the first time, and described him with utmost praise as 'beautiful' and 'sexy, like an animal.' Nobody else had analysed him before like Angela did, when she said, 'He wriggles his whole body like a penis.' It was quite an accurate comment, I think. She was not interested in his songs or in his voice at all. Although irrelevant, I said, 'Elvis's performance on stage, especially the way he shuffles his legs and lowers his hips with legs wide open when he looks at the audience is very similar to a *kabuki* performance called "*mie,*"[11] don't you think?' Angela said, 'It's probably a coincidence, but I heard he practices *karate*, so perhaps he has seen a photo of a *kabuki* actor doing "*mie.*"' Angela was uncharacteristically well-informed in this matter.

I do not remember when it was exactly during that winter, but in Shinjuku I came across a friend whom I had often met up with in town. He told me one of our mutual friends had tried to commit suicide because of a broken heart, although the attempt had been unsuccessful. He also told us that another friend, a girl we often saw in town, had killed her live-in boyfriend and been arrested. He had some more minor news that so-and-so had been employed by a company and quit

---

[11] *Mie*: a typical *kabuki* posture in which a *kabuki* actor holds his pose at a critical point to exaggerate his gesture.

'*Mie*' in *kabuki* performance

his Shinjuku life, and that so-and-so had started to live with so-and-so with the idea of one day getting married, and had started working diligently.

It was only a few months that we were away from Shinjuku, but already so many things had happened to my friends and acquaintances. Hearing all those things, I was gripped with an anxiety that I might have been missing something critical while I was enjoying the quiet life with Angela at our cottage in Kujukuri. The winter was almost over, however, and the day of our return to Tokyo from our seaside paradise, the end of our life in the country, was fast approaching.

Angela's Attitude toward Sex and Her Sexual Conduct

So far, I have written about the daily occurrences and incidents that took place in my life with Angela Carter, which lasted for over a year. I wrote as they came back to me, in a fragmentary and disorderly manner. All the while, however, I have avoided mentioning two elements that I think might be very important in understanding Angela Carter as a fiction writer. These two elements seem too significant to mention in passing, thus I feel the need to write about them in an organized way. Also, to tell the truth, I have been reluctant to write about these two topics, and wished not to touch upon them, if possible.

What are these two elements, then? One of them is Angela Carter's view on sex and her sexual conduct. Those of you who have read Angela Carter's literary works know that her works are occupied with a powerful sexual imagination, and without understanding her view on sex, one cannot fully grasp her works. I will begin with the easiest part, and write about how Angela used to assess literary descriptions of sex, to the extent that I can remember.

In respect to such descriptions, she regarded D.H. Lawrence highly. She said, holding my hand and looking into my eyes, 'Lawrence was trying to say that what life is all about is this communication between bodies, intercourse between flesh.' She told me this three or four times. 'That's a matter of course, isn't it?' I said, though I was struck by the fact that not many writers in Japan ever actually wrote it down. Angela said, 'Lawrence was the first person in England to address it directly.' The reason why she appreciated Jun'ichiro Tanizaki so much must have been because she appreciated his depictions and conceptualisation of sex. She admired the nonchalant relationship between the married couple described in *The Key*,[12] and the subtle relationship with the mistress in *Some Prefer Nettles*,[13] saying, 'Tanizaki understands that a couple is formed by two strangers, male and female, and how they remain strangers even as they are married. He deals with matters between a married couple as in a romantic story.' She also spoke highly of the romance in *A Portrait of Shunkin*,[14] and of the sexuality of the elderly in *Diary of a Mad Old Man*,[15] as a further demonstration of Freud's psychoanalysis.

She showed little interest in Kawabata's description of sex, saying sarcastically, 'His love will be complete when he

---

[12] Tanizaki's novel, published in 1956.

[13] Tanizaki's novel, published in 1929.

[14] Tanizaki's novel, published in 1933.

[15] Tanizaki's novel, published in 1961.

makes a lover out of a doll.' She spoke ill of Henry Miller and Norman Mailer, popular in Japan in those days, saying, 'They're just dirty and filthy.'

Interestingly, she did not talk about Marquis de Sade in terms of sexual issues, such as sadism or masochism. She said, 'He probably wanted to say that those with stronger energy conquer those with weaker energy.'

It has nothing to do with literature, but Angela worked as a hostess at a bar in Ginza for two weeks, and wrote an article based on this experience in *Josei Jishin*, a Japanese weekly tabloid journal for women. Around that time, she asked me, 'What do you think Japanese men are paying a lot of money for when they visit those bars? You know, those hardworking men who sacrifice their lives for corporations.' I said, 'To court women, of course, right?' She said, 'You would think so, wouldn't you? In fact, no, that's not it.' 'Then, for what?' I asked. Angela said, 'They pay outrageous prices in order to play kindergarten. Do you see now? They don't come to court women or to seduce women, they come to return to a kindergarten state and be coddled. In this strange kindergarten for grown-up men, hostesses are required to simulate the role of a kindergarten teacher. If you perform well as a teacher, you earn a lot.' She said to me, 'Having seen the interactions at bars between hostesses and customers, I came to better understand the essence of the literature of Saikaku Ihara (an author in the Edo period, famous for *The Life of an Amorous Man*, and *Five Women Who Loved Love*), and Kafu Nagai (an author active in the Meiji to Showa eras).'

Angela had a keen interest in Kafu Nagai, who spent his life at bars, whorehouses, and striptease clubs. Her interest in him was not directed at him as a writer, but as an individual, as a man. On the other hand, she came to ridicule the Japanese businessmen who regularly haunted Ginza bars, and she looked upon them with pity and intense dislike.

It probably goes without saying, but she talked about many more writers, especially British and European writers from the Middle Ages and Early Modern period, and about the way they described romantic relationships and sex. But alas, because of my lack of knowledge, I could not understand what or whom she was talking about, and therefore, I remember very little.

We may need to move on from Angela's assessment of literary works and their descriptions of love and sex to her personal views on sex and sexual conduct in her own life. (I am still hesitant to write what I am going to write here. It is difficult to suppress the doubt regarding whether I should write this far, considering what Angela Carter herself might have felt about it.)

When I slept with her for the first time, she said, 'I just lie on my back and stay still.' To be sure, she was discreet. As we went through many nights together, though, she became more expressive, but she was still, as I recall, on the modest side.

Upon returning to Japan after going back to England and us beginning our life in the Meguro flat, Angela started to change. Around that time, she became oddly enticed by young

Japanese women. She would sit in a tea room and observe each and every one of the girls in the room and on the outside street. At first, she would say positive things about them like, 'No young women in Japan are ugly. They are all pretty and cute, if not beautiful. They look so happy and cheerful that it puts you in a good mood.' Gradually, however, she began to say negative things. 'It is disagreeable when a grown-up woman giggles like a schoolgirl.' 'They pretend to be shy when there is nothing to be shy about. I bet they act naïve and weak to attract men's attention.' 'So silly that they imitate the white race by dyeing their hair blond. The era of the whites has already reached its end.' Though their relationship was coincidental, the more Angela came to speak ill of Japanese women, the more she became expressive and active during sex. She would touch and often lick every corner of my body, saying things a Japanese woman would never dare to say, such as, 'Your skin feels so nice and smooth,' or, 'You are beautiful and slender like a young boy,' or, 'Your muscles are as pliant and supple as an animal.' Her compliments did not make me feel bad, of course, but they did not particularly please me either, to tell the truth. I just thought, 'She talks a lot,' and was a bit embarrassed. That was all. Of course, compliments were better than negative put-downs.

As Angela began to praise my body and face in a more direct manner, she also became more active, voluntarily exposing more of her naked body to me, demanding more insistently to be loved by me. Perhaps her curiosity was stirred by the illustrations she saw in some Japanese S&M stories, because she began asking me to tie her up or whip her. I had no interest in S&M, so I refused her half-serious request by telling her jokingly, 'You're asking for too much. Things need to be kept in moderation, you see.' Thereafter, the possibility of S&M disappeared.

All the other flats in our apartment building in Meguro were occupied by Caucasians. Right next to us lived a round-faced, plump English man, who looked very good-natured, the sort of Caucasian guy typically seen in movies. A young Japanese woman came to visit him about twice a week. I did not see her myself, but Angela described her as 'young.' Although I never saw her face, I heard her voice often. The building was cheaply built and its walls were thin, so the noise next door was completely audible.

At about six o'clock in the evening, we heard a voice of a woman, though we could not make out what she was saying. Then we heard a lower male voice, and their subdued conversation afterwards. A period of silence, then there came the woman's panting. This was repeated about twice a week. I used to come home deliberately around the time she came to visit the room next door, and would open the closet door and wait for her panting to begin. As a matter of course, Angela also came to notice the sighing, panting, and shouting from the neighbouring room in no time.

Once, while we were listening to the voice from next door, Angela said, 'That girl might be the kind of girl who faints.' I did not know that some women lost consciousness during sex, so I asked, 'Is such a thing possible?' Angela replied, 'For some women, yes.'

Aroused by the noise from next door, we often began to make love ourselves, though it was still light outside. I soon began to realize, after many sessions like this, Angela got more excited than usual with the stimulation from our next-door neighbours. Then, one day, when we were resting our sweaty bodies after sex, Angela abruptly said, 'I want to see our neighbours having sex.' When I asked, 'Do you really want to see that white English pig flopping about?' she said, 'Not at all, that would make me sick. I want to see the Japanese girl panting.' Then she continued, 'I want to see a Japanese girl's naked body having sex, her face in ecstasy, her lips in particular.' I realized from Angela's expression that she was not joking.

It was certain that Angela was sexually aroused by the erotic image of a Japanese girl. Judging from the fragmentary words she uttered, a chubby, healthy-looking girl with a darker skin pigment aroused her imagination the most. I do not really think Angela had a lesbian tendency, though, because Angela did not seem to have the desire to be emotionally connected to women, the kind of desire that is found in lesbians, in my opinion.

A small incident occurred in September at the end of the 'crazy' summer, which urged Angela and me to act as we did. I came to know a young woman when I was out with my mates in Shinjuku, and slept with her once or twice at a hotel. Angela found a lipstick mark on my underwear. Reluctant to tell her that I chatted up a woman at a bar and went to a hotel,

I quickly made up a story and told Angela that I had caught the eye of a young girl on the train and when I talked to her, she came along and gave me a blowjob in a park.

This made-up story seemed to excite her fantasies. After that, whenever Angela saw a girl alone on an empty train, she would say to me delightedly, 'If you were by yourself, you would ask her out, wouldn't you?' Angela began dropping hints that I should seduce a young woman.

It was soon after this small incident and my small lie, as I remember. One evening, when a cool breeze had started blowing, Angela and I were drinking beer at a place – something between a café and a bar – near Meguro station. To be honest, I am not sure if it was really near Meguro station. It was certainly not in Shinjuku. The whole thing seems like a dream in my memory now. I do not have a clear recollection of it, but somehow we were talking with a young woman. The girl was twenty-one or twenty-two years of age, average height for a Japanese girl, with sunburned skin from seemingly having spent the summer at the beach, and a thick stature. She giggled a lot while drinking beer. In her broken English mixed with Japanese, she told us that she was a student of early childhood education and a model, as well. Not a slim fashion model, but a model for advertisements for flower shops, bakeries, and the like. She said she was going to work at a kindergarten when she graduated.

She admired Angela half-drunkenly, saying, 'You're beautiful,' 'You have nice long legs, like a model,' and 'Your hair is gorgeous.' She then asked what Angela did for a living, and when she learned that Angela was a writer, she said, 'Wow, you're so smart,' praising Angela even more. She was a girl with an atmosphere both mature and childish at the same time. That was all that transpired. A short while later, the girl left us, saying, 'See you again.'

However, the girl did not leave Angela's imagination. In front of the girl, Angela did nothing but sit and smile. She did not compliment the girl or ask her questions. Actually, she said nothing at all. However, when we returned to our flat that evening, she kept on talking about the girl, and to my surprise, told me that she wanted to see me having sex with the girl. When I look back now, Angela's feelings were not so much those of sexual desire, but rather, curiosity.

It was a week or so after that day. One night in a jazz café in Kabuki-cho, we met Yuko. Yuko was twenty-three years old then (if she was telling the truth, that is), and was similar to the girl we had met at the bar in Meguro. She was plump with tanned skin, talked a lot in Japanese mixed with broken English, and giggled constantly. We laughed a lot and drank a lot of beer, just as we did in Meguro.

Yuko said she was also a model. Not a fashion model, but mostly for bust shots, she said. Without a doubt, she did not look like a fashion model, though her face could be described as photogenic. She said she was studying graphic design. 'Modelling does not last long, you see,' said Yuko, adding, 'I work at a disco twice a week.' She was one of the numerous young women in Tokyo who were beautiful and attractive to a certain degree, and had some modest dreams and ambitions.

When Yuko learned that Angela was a novelist, she said, 'Wow, you're amazing,' and seemed to be impressed. She praised Angela's looks, too, and acted coquettishly to both Angela and me, giggling a lot and smiling charmingly. She bought us beer. In return, we bought her a cocktail.

After several more rounds, we got drunk. When I complimented Yuko saying, 'You're pretty' and 'You're sexy,' Angela did the same. When I touched Yuko's long black hair, Angela, far from stopping me, urged me to touch her more daringly. What was probably in her mind occurred to me then, but I was still perplexed. Nonetheless, I reached for Yuko's shoulder and said to her, 'You have beautiful skin.' Yuko admired my hands and hair and smiled, then giggled.

Similar to the girl we had met at the café in Meguro, Yuko had an atmosphere that combined the maturity of an older woman, as well as the childishness peculiar to young Japanese women. At one moment, she showed the consideration of a grown-up woman, and at another, she behaved and looked like a girl of fourteen or fifteen years old. Looking back, I think Angela was strangely attracted to this quality that Japanese women exuded, of maturity and childishness mixed in an odd balance. She might have found the peculiar coexistence of child and adult in them repulsive, as well as erotic. The immature behaviour and expressions of Japanese women repelled her, probably because she considered them to be proof that they were not liberated as women, and that they did not take responsibility for their lives as grown-up human beings. She might also have taken their childish manners and expressions as a cover for their lack of will and independence. Certainly, Angela was always criticising them with a similar logic.

According to my fragmented memory, Yuko, Angela, and I left the jazz bar in Kabuki-cho, got in a taxi, and headed for Meguro. At first, we were just giving Yuko a lift to her apartment near Shimokitazawa.[19] Somehow along the way, we changed our destination to Meguro while we were in the taxi. I remember Angela whispered in my ear, 'Invite her to Meguro,' and I replied 'OK,' anticipating that something exciting would happen.

As we entered the room, we sat on the *tatami* floor, and poured some leftover *sake* from a bottle stored in our kitchen, and drank it. The *sake* went quickly, so we drank some whiskey and water afterwards. Or so I remember… Everything is so hazy now. Perhaps it was another occasion on which we drank *sake* and whiskey. Because it happened forty years ago, things are mixed up and buried deep down in my memory.

The three of us became very drunk. Or, perhaps, it was only Yuko and I that got drunk, and Angela was not drunk at all. For, though Angela would not stop me from drinking alcohol, she usually drank very little herself, and I had never seen her drunk.

I am not sure how things proceeded, but after a while, Yuko said, 'I'll give you a striptease.' She abruptly turned off the light in the *tatami* room so that the only light was from the kitchen, and she began the show. As she sang a melody, she took out a sheet or a large towel from the cupboard, and using it as a stage prop, she began to step, swing her hips, and dance. As she danced, she took off her clothes piece by piece. The way she did it did not look like an amateur imitation. It was airy, rhythmical, and suggestive. Perhaps Yuko had worked as a stripper before.

I cannot say for sure if what I write next actually happened. It may have been a wild fantasy that stuck to some part of my brain as a memory. My memory of Yuko seems too vivid and too detailed to be natural, if it were real.

Anyway, in my memory, Yuko wrapped a sheet around her body, and took off all her clothes with ease: first her skirt, then blouse, underwear, stockings. Then she laid down on her back on the *tatami* mats, wriggled her hips under the sheet to show her thigh a little. When I reached out to touch her thigh, she showed us her nipple. When Angela touched it, Yuko removed the sheet from her belly to reveal her private parts.

My memory of what we did afterwards is blurry. It seems that Yuko and I started to fumble at each other, after which Angela joined in, and we spent a raucous night together. I was too drunk to say for sure what we did, except that the next morning, we saw Yuko off at the station as the sun was rising. Yuko was in high spirits on the way of the station, and talked about movies and novels the whole way.

We never saw Yuko again after that. Angela and I talked to another young girl, a cosmetic shop clerk, at the same jazz café in Kabuki-cho, and invited her to our apartment in Meguro as before. However, the girl flatly refused to be sexually approached by me or by Angela, and wanted only to talk until the next morning. We did not feel like doing anything further in the face of the girl's strong resistance. Violent acts were out of the question. After a while, Angela fell asleep, and I talked about various things with the girl until morning, and when she left, I saw her off to the street near the station.

For a while, Angela and I kept on talking about having a threesome with a young Japanese girl, and said jokingly, 'Why don't we try it again?' But we never had the chance, and then we moved to Kujukuri, leaving Tokyo behind. At our seaside cottage, our wild fancy was revived from time to time, and we occasionally mentioned threesomes. Such an outrageous pleasure was impossible in a seaside village, however. We rarely saw young women in the first place.

I am certain that Angela had an intense, erotic feeling toward young Japanese women. Yet at the same time, she eternally scorned them, and often positively despised them. In short, it may be the case that Angela found young Japanese women all the more erotic precisely because she scorned and despised them. To be certain, I think that the stronger your scorn and disgust for an object is, the stronger your erotic feelings toward it become. I found these illogical contradictions in Angela's attitude not only in regard to young Japanese women, but to sex in general. Having said that, I do not think this attitude makes Angela a particularly contradictory woman. For almost no human beings are exempt from contradictory attitudes toward sex.

How is Angela's contradictory attitude toward sex, of which her feelings for young Japanese women are exemplary, reflected in her novels? To me, it seems to be ingrained in many parts of Angela's novels, but I think the task of answering that question in detail needs to be left in the hands of Carter's more ardent readers and critics. As for me, I will just write down what I myself witnessed her saying and doing, as someone who was by her side at that time.

Chapter 6

The Psychology of Stutterers

I wrote what I knew first-hand about Angela Carter's sexual conduct and her views on sex, only because I thought it would offer an important clue to understanding her literary works. However, I purposely left one other factor untouched until now, which I believe is even more significant in understanding her works. It is the fact that Angela Carter had a severe stutter.

When we met for the first time and talked for about an hour at Fugetsudo in Shinjuku, I suspected her to be a stutterer. It was not only because she stumbled several times when trying to say something and stuttered slightly, but also because she had the kind of speech peculiar to a stutterer: a hardness, as if something was stuck in her throat, and an instability that broke down the smooth rhythm of speech. Naturally, people often stumble or stutter when saying something, even if they are not a real stutterer. In the case of Angela, however, the way her voice did not come out smoothly, as if the throat were blocked, and the way it lost its rhythm in the beginning or in the middle of the sentence, was unique to a true stutterer. Of course, I found these typical characteristics of a stutterer in Angela only because I myself was one, too.

What kind of personality and character traits does a stutterer have? Or, put differently, what kind of a person, or more accurately, what kind of a child, with what personality and character traits, becomes a stutterer? I put the question this way, because most stutterers become stutterers in their childhood.

It is generally believed that a shy, passive, quiet, and unsociable child who is not good at making friends becomes a stutterer, triggered by a painful experience such as bullying. Most people say so when talking about stuttering. Nothing is further away from reality than this generally held belief, though many may be surprised to hear it. Most children who later become stutterers are the opposite of the kind of children depicted in this common view.

In most cases, a stutterer, since the time he or she is still an infant and therefore not a full stutterer yet, is talkative, friendly, sociable, and active, far from being quiet, withdrawn, unsociable, or passive. He or she is not talkative in the sociable and friendly sense, rather in the sense that he or she is very self-assertive, eagerly wanting to express his or her opinion and to debate with others. He or she is a child who is always impatient to articulate as fast as possible what he or she thinks and feels. Importantly, when he or she speaks quickly, it is unlike the way many girls chatter quickly in a smooth, rhythmical, and flowing manner. His or her speech becomes jerky, because the speed is much too fast, and it loses its rhythm and smoothness.

Also contrary to the general view, most stutterers are open-minded, friendly, frank even to strangers, and can talk to anybody. A typical and extreme example of a stutterer is the late Kakuei Tanaka,[1] ex-Prime Minister of Japan, which also might be a surprise to most readers. Kakuei Tanaka, who suffered from a serious case of stuttering, deduced that if he stuttered, the stuttering must come from the way he spoke and not from his weak-heartedness or timidity, because he was far from being weak-hearted, and had never been afraid to talk in public. In an attempt to correct his way of speaking, he learned to sing traditional ditties from a teacher. Through these ditties, he tried to master slow breathing and slow vocalization. By practicing these ditties, he learned to pace his rhythm by tapping a *sensu*[2] as he talked, and consequently, it became a speaking style that was unique to Kakuei Tanaka. Originally, these breathing and speaking methods were used to overcome his stuttering, but he made use of them in order to wade through the political world, where speech is a weapon. As a result, he made it to the top.

Let us recall the way Kakuei Tanaka spoke and behaved. He always talked impatiently and quickly, asserting his opinion without really listening to others. The way he talked was

---

[1] Kakuei Tanaka: Japan's Prime Minister from 1972-74. He was the head of the Liberal Democratic Party of Japan in its height, and famous for his strong speeches. He was arrested in relation to the Lockheed bribery scandal and was found guilty, but died in 1993 before the final verdict was handed down by the Supreme Court.

[2] *Sensu*: a small folding fan used as a prop on stage by entertainers of Edo classical art.

not at all gentle, nor smooth, nor rhythmical, but always hasty and urgent. Yet, he maintained an overall comical atmosphere, and looked as if he were always in a good mood, as if he genuinely enjoyed meeting people.

What I found in Angela Carter were characteristics similar to the ones Kakuei Tanaka had. Angela always talked fast about what was on her mind, in a frank, impatient, and urgent manner. She generally seemed to enjoy meeting and talking to new people (on the condition that they spoke English), and often ended up starting passionate debates with them. She had a comical atmosphere, perhaps because of her frank and straightforward manner.

The Distress of Stutterers

What sort of distress or handicap does stuttering inflict on a stutterer? How do they feel in their daily lives as a consequence? Pointblank, being a stutterer is painful. The distress of a stutterer is close to my heart, as I myself have been stuttering all my life, as far as I can remember, since I was five or six. Let me share with you the testimonies made by other stutterers on how painful their lives can be:

'I don't remember when I began to stutter, but I clearly remember that I was stuttering when I entered elementary school. School life was fun, but torture at the same time. Whenever I happened to stutter, my close friends would laugh at me and ridicule me, so I was always scared of being called on and stuttering. Reading class was especially horrifying whenever my turn to read aloud approached. I stopped stuttering shortly after I became a junior high student. Since then, I have forgotten the pain of stuttering. But recently, at forty years of age, the fear I felt as a student came back to me. I have nightmares these days. I am scared and wake up sweating.' (Surgeon, male, age forty-five)

'I was working in a sales section, but got fired again last week. The order I received was for seventy-five cases, but I couldn't say "*nanaju*"[3] because it made me stutter, so I reported that the order was for sixty-five cases. By that point, I had already been reprimanded several times, because I kept putting in wrong orders. One thing led to another, and I was fired again.' (Office worker, male, age twenty-eight)

'I run a company, and on the first day of every month, I give an admonitory speech in front of all my employees. However, this speech is such an effort because I stutter. I am relieved when I deliver the speech and the first day of the month is gone, but the anxiety starts to mount from the middle of the month, and the last week of the month is so terrifying that I cannot work properly. Yet, the president's admonitory speech is important for my business, so I cannot do away with it. If I stop doing it, it means I've lost the battle…. The end of the month is approaching again. It is terrifying. (Company president, male, age forty-six)

'How do I live as a stutterer? Nothing helps, no matter if I

---

[3] '*Nanaju*' equates to seventy. Seventy-five in Japanese is '*nanaju-go.*' Sixty-five is '*rokuju-go.*'

study, do lots of extracurricular activities, or try to be fashionable. Even if I make myself beautiful, it is all spoiled as soon as I open my mouth. Even if I am dressed in the latest fashion, if I happen to reveal my stuttering and show how I distort my face and twitch my throat and lips, how can a boy fall in love with me?' (Student, female, age eighteen)

These testimonies are only a small part of what stutterers themselves have told me in person or have written to me in letters, when, in my early forties, I involved myself in the issues surrounding stuttering. Then again, they attest to the fact that these are only the tip of the iceberg when it comes to the terrible effects of the disorder called stuttering. Stuttering does not only cause inconveniences because one cannot speak smoothly or communicate well. To stutter as a chronic sufferer of this disorder – not as an occasional stutterer who happens to stumble upon words – means a defeat in the mind of the stutterer. When he or she stutters, all sorts of negative feelings roar inside a chronic stutterer, and he or she feels embarrassed, ugly, defeated, anxious, terrified, impatient, desperate, inferior, helpless, lonely, and so on and so forth. To that extent, stuttering is a painful, negative, and terrible condition.

That pain, for most people, is beyond the limit a person can bear. What does one do, when one finds an element in oneself that is too disagreeable, painful, and terrible to accept? Surely he or she would try to eliminate that negative, distressing, terrible element. Yet, when he or she fails to eliminate it, what does he or she do? He or she would try to convince him or herself that the aforementioned disagreeable element does not exist in him or herself at all, and behave accordingly. In short, stutterers act as if they have nothing to do with stuttering. Thus, they do not touch on the topic of stuttering.

What if, somehow, one had to face the fact that one was a stutterer? Interestingly, one would try very hard to appear nonchalant about it, saying to oneself, if not to others, that he or she certainly stutters a little, but he or she is not worried about it at all, that a little stutter does not bother him or her.

I think these kinds of self-deceiving thoughts and conduct are what one generally adopts when he or she feels inferior.

Kenzaburo Oe and Somerset Maugham

Regarding the tendency of stuttering to trap its sufferer in a sense of his or her own inferiority, I will present two examples; both of them are famous novelists.

The Nobel Prize in Literature winner Kenzaburo Oe has never written on the topic of his own stuttering, even though he is a serious stutterer. Though he has continually written on the issue of inferiority complexes, and on the disability of his son in detail, I have never read anything Oe wrote about his stuttering. (Though I must say, I have not read his later works. I have only read the works he wrote up until his forties.)

Another famous stutterer is Somerset Maugham, also a novelist. In his novel, *Of Human Bondage,*[4] Maugham writes about a tragic man cursed by disability, who may well be

---
[4] A novel written by William Somerset Maugham, published in 1915.

modelled after the author himself. However, the author gave the protagonist a bad leg, not a stuttering condition. (By the way, the Japanese translation of the title, *Ningen-no-Kizuna*, is a problematic translation, I think, because '*kizuna*' in Japanese is similar to, yet quite distinct from, 'bondage.')[5]

It is mere speculation, but I think Maugham must have tried to create a young protagonist burdened with a disability out of his own painful experience of stuttering. Yet, he probably could not bring himself to write about stuttering in detail, because he would have been reminded of his own embarrassing, disgusting, and painful experiences. So instead, he must have fabricated a young man with another disability, i.e. a bad leg.

As I am penning this, I realize that the real distress of a stuttering disorder is that it is not considered a handicap, and is a target of ridicule and mockery, because a stutterer looks unsightly, comical, and extremely timid. In other words, it dawned on me that the real terror of a stuttering disorder might be the fact that it invites thoughtless mockery and ridicule, and these things, in spite of their superficiality and childishness, can shatter human pride so easily and completely.

Angela Carter as a Stutterer

I have been tormented by this devil called stuttering for as

---

[5] Araki is suggesting that the translator might have mistaken the word 'bondage' as 'bond,' the Japanese translation of which is '*kizuna*.' To be sure, '*kizuna*' does not mean 'bondage' in this sense, that is, 'to be bound' or 'be under restraint/captivity.'

long as I can remember. I wonder how it was for Angela, who was also a stutterer. She frequently stuttered. Whenever she went shopping, ordered at a restaurant, or greeted people, she stumbled over her words and stuttered. She did so even when she was relaxed, talking with me while lying on the *tatami* floor, or in bed.

Usually when she stuttered, she would mumble some words under her breath, and repeat the same sound once or twice. It was fairly unnoticeable to those who were not stutterers themselves. Sometimes, however, when we were talking with each other, she stuttered so hard she had trouble breathing. On such occasions, I would put my hand on her shoulder gently, bring her a glass of water, or rub her back, as if she had had some kind of fit. When she was talking with her British friends and stumbled over her words and stuttered, they often teased her or stifled their smiles.

Though she herself was a severe stutterer, she once pointed out that I stuttered and said, 'But it's not important. You don't need to worry about it.'

I am not sure how much Angela was tormented by her own stuttering. I do not know whether she even minded it or not. I never asked her about her stuttering, and she never told me about it herself. Once, when she was talking on the phone to either an American or an English friend, she described herself as a 'Truman Capote-esque woman.' A giantess who stutters appears in *Breakfast at Tiffany's*, and I think she drew on this giantess to describe herself as a stutterer.

I remember one time when she was talking with a white

woman, most probably a tourist from England, at a café in Shinjuku, and she stuttered more than usual. She then said to the woman, 'I can't teach English because I stutter like this.' Once when she was talking to John, John laughed at her as she choked on saying a word, 'a, a, a….' Then, I remember, she chided him, saying, 'It's not fair to laugh at the disabilities of others.'

Though we stuttered daily in our life together, I never spoke about stuttering, and neither did Angela. It is odd when I think about it. This odd fact in itself seems to prove how deeply we were troubled by this disorder. It may only be my imagination. And yet, perhaps, though Angela was tormented in her mind as much as I was, she might have pretended to feel no pain whatsoever, and to live without ever talking about it, as if she had nothing to do with stuttering, even though she stuttered many times every single day.

Suppose I had asked Angela how it really was for her, when we were living together forty years ago; I do not think it would have turned out to be a meaningful conversation, because Angela probably would have replied, 'I don't mind it at all. It's not really important.'

And yet, even if she had denied it, I never would have believed a word of it. Especially in today's social climate, in which women have obtained a certain social status that comes with responsibility, and are required in turn to be able to speak well in public. Such an ability is considered a major feminine charm (as proved by the popularity of female announcers and reporters, not only in terms of their careers, but also as prospective brides); thus, I do not believe any woman with a handicap that prevents her from speaking well can avoid feeling shame, a sense of inferiority, chagrin, or self-hatred, particularly when she knows what to say in her head perfectly but cannot utter it because of her stammering.

Thinking about this, I am reminded of the time when I asked Angela why she got married so young, when she was just twenty years old. Angela said, 'I thought I would never be able to get married if I didn't accept the proposal.' At that time, I took her words lightly, thinking, 'When we are young, we often feel that way.' But what she might have had in mind then was, 'No other person will ever want to marry such an unattractive, stuttering girl.' Most stutterers believe in their minds that nobody can love them because they stutter so awkwardly. They think, 'Nobody will love me once they know I am a stutterer.'

However, the reality is often contrary to what stutterers fear. Because of the upbeat and frank personality unique to stutterers, or perhaps because their awareness of their own inferiority makes them subconsciously sympathetic to others, most of them are popular among men and women.[6]

---

[6] In fact, Carter mentions Sozo's stutter in her journal in an affectionate tone. We cannot fathom how she viewed her own stutter, but at least she was moved by the fact that she and Sozo shared the condition. See "Her Side of the Story."

The Making of a Stutterer

What triggers a child to turn into a stutterer? Not all children who speak quickly and urgently become stutterers. Looking at children around the age of four or five, you can find many with bad speech habits, some hasty and restless. Only a small number of them become stutterers, however; most children with bad speech habits go through youth and grow up without becoming stutterers.

It seems to me, in addition to bad speech habits and a restless personality, what makes a child a stutterer is a shock from the outside that preys on his or her mind, a painful experience of anxiety and terror; that is, a strong stressor that torments the child. Only after a painful event or stressful experience will a child with the typical constitution of a stutterer become a real stutterer, it seems.

When I became a stutterer at the age of five or six, my parents were on the verge of getting a divorce, and they quarrelled almost every day. Their shouts, my father's violence against my mother, and the night my mother finally left and did not return…. In such an environment that world plant anxiety and fear in my tender heart, I turned into a stutterer.

I overcame stuttering when I was around the third grade in elementary school, but then our family moved to a farming village, a totally different environment from what I had been used to, and I had to attend a new school with a new set of rules. Also, my father's new wife joined our family, and new tension, new arguments, and new anxieties were introduced.

Due to that environment, I began to stutter again.

I wonder how it was for Angela Carter. In what environment did she grow up, and what made her a stutterer? We never talked about anything related to stuttering at all. I never asked her about it, and she never spoke about it. I do not think she neglected mentioning it because she did not mind her own stuttering. I myself never spoke about my stuttering or anything related to it to anybody, and pretended that I had no such unsightly disability. I did not show anyone the distress I felt.

In fact, when I involved myself in a treatment program for stutterers in my forties and started to talk about the pain and hardship I had experienced as a stutterer, all of my friends were surprised and said to me, 'We never imagined that Araki suffered from such a disorder,' or, 'I didn't realize you stuttered,' or, 'You were always easy-going, like you had no worries in the world.'

Angela told me about her family and parents, and how she had grown up. She described her father as 'a gentle man, a kind person,' and seemed to adore him. On the other hand, she appeared to rather hate her mother (though I did not think of it as odd, because I thought every mother and daughter were rivals and bound to hate each other). Angela often described her mother as 'pathologically sensitive,' or 'pathologically fastidious,' and told me about rather unbelievable episodes, which could very well be figments of Angela's imagination, such as 'I used to be reprimanded so severely that I was confined in a dark cupboard when I was little,' or 'When I reached puberty, she checked my underwear every night for traces of semen.'

As I write this, trying to recollect the short period of time we shared, I can hardly remember her telling me about her youthful days, her student days. Right after we came to know each other in Shinjuku, I took her to the university I graduated from, and I remember that she, uninterested in the university, only said to me, 'My university days were not fun at all. I don't have any good memories of them.'

This is, of course, only my personal speculation, but I think that Angela's only enjoyment during her dark adolescent days was to read books and write stories. I imagine she was finally liberated when she won some literary awards and was recognized as a young, professional novelist. It is not that I think this way in retrospect; I felt this way already when I was living with Angela.

When I was counselling a female stutterer, she said to me, 'A stutterer's life is like living in a dark room where the door is only slightly ajar.' What she described in those words and Angela Carter's young days, with which I am personally unfamiliar, may have been similar.

Perhaps I should stop writing uncertain things from my imagination, though. Surely, we can find in the literary works that Angela Carter left behind certain characteristics peculiar to stutterers, such as vivacity, positivity, power, humour, kindness, generosity, and yet also all the opposite qualities, such as anxiety, terror, impatience, childish narcissism, self-hatred, and animosity toward others. Of course, as I previously stated, an evaluation of her literature should not be done lightly by someone like me who has a limited ability in English, but should be carried out by literary scholars, Japanese or otherwise, who can pick up on the delicate nuances of English.

Chapter 7

Angela's Brief Return to England

To be honest about how I felt during the composition of this memoir, I quite enjoyed it when I began writing, and up until the middle part, I was light-hearted. However, a heaviness gradually crept over me, and when I came to the topic of Angela's sexuality and her stuttering, I was almost too tormented to go on. As the pain increased, I was only able to write if I proceeded extremely slowly.

It was a painful task, not only because I had to expose my own sense of inferiority; I was constantly bothered by the thought, 'Angela wouldn't be happy to know I wrote this much.' And yet, if I wanted to write something remotely meaningful about Angela Carter, it goes without saying that I needed to write what pained me, including what I might be reluctant to write about, as truthfully as possible.

What I am going to write from now on is even more painful to me, because I need to write more about myself – my insincerity, my immaturity, and my weakness – than about Angela Carter. Also, it is unavoidable that I, yet again, must face how Angela must have felt during the last few months of our life together, of which I do not want to be reminded.

Under such circumstances, these last pages until the end will be a brief report of what happened between us, in chronological order. Angela and I did not spend much time together the year after we moved from the seaside cottage. I cannot, therefore, do anything but write mainly about what happened to me, in order to complete this memoir. When Angela Carter is pushed into the background, it will be of little interest to the reader, so it is also advisable to keep this section as brief as possible.

At the end of March or the beginning of April that year, Angela and I left the seaside cottage in Kujukuri and returned to Tokyo.[1] While we temporarily stayed at my brother's residence or Angela's friend John's apartment, I looked for a place to live and for a job, and Angela prepared for her return to England. While we were staying at my brother's, my brother happened to be away for his job. Thus, while Angela did not have a chance to meet him, she frequently talked with his wife, who was ill, and became close to their children. She taught them how to paint, and she read them children's books in English. Surrounded by my family, Angela was 'Aunty Angela'; she was always frank, friendly, kind, and intelligent.

She also met my father, who happened to visit us there. Angela, with the help of my interpretation, talked with him about many topics, such as Chaucer and the fall of the British Empire. Angela and my father were both very amicable to one another, which made me imagine how Angela might have spoken to Soseki Natsume if she had met him.

---

[1] According to Gordon, they returned to Tokyo on 29 March, 1971 (p. 179).

I do not remember what day in April it was, but Angela left for England from Haneda Airport, saying she was coming back to Japan right away. She said that she would divorce her husband officially. Her husband was living with a young woman, so there should have been no problem. If I remember correctly, she was wearing the same dress she had worn when she arrived in Japan a year earlier, and disappeared smiling through the departure gate. She looked very relaxed, contrary to one year prior.

The Tragic Trial Lecture

I rented a small room not even three *tatami* mats wide near Shin-Nakano[2] station, and found a job as a day-worker in Takadanobaba.[3] I worked during the day and went out to Shinjuku in the evenings, as before. I met with my buddies, whom I had not seen for a while because I had been out of Tokyo. We gossiped about people we knew, and talked about our dreams and many other things over glasses of beer. I was still full of energy and ambition, and I did not have any worries about the future.

After spending about a week or so like this, I thought I needed to find a more stable job, and started looking for one. I found an advertisement for a job as an English teacher at a

---

[2] Shin-Nakano: the third stop from Shinjuku on the Marunouchi subway line (to the west of Shinjuku).

[3] Takadanobaba: the second stop from Shinjuku on the JR Yamanote line (to the north of Shinjuku).

cram school, and decided to give it try. Unfortunately, on my first day of job hunting, tragedy struck. To call it a tragedy may be an improper use of the word, but for me, it was nothing but a tragedy.

It was on the evening of a fine day in April. I went for an interview at a cram school in Ogikubo.[4] I took a simple English paper exam, and then was asked to give a trial lecture on relative pronouns to third graders in junior high school.[5]

I was all right up until halfway through the lecture, though I stuttered from time to time. Whenever I stuttered, seven or eight students would giggle, but it was of no serious consequence. However, when I had to call the class roll, I suddenly began to stutter severely. I went on calling names through my stutter, but at a certain name, my voice stopped coming out entirely. It was an ordinary name, Hayashi or something, if I remember correctly. Standing petrified in front of the class, I desperately tried to vocalize the sound '*ha*,' writhing my body and swinging my arms. However, the sound I attempted to make did not come out; it was stuck in the back of my throat. The students guffawed at me. The headmaster and the other employees of the school laughed a little, then stopped laughing completely and stared at me in consternation.

Each stutterer has a unique set of sounds that he or she

---

[4] Ogikubo: the sixth stop from Shinjuku on the JR Chuo line (to the west of Shinjuku).

[5] In the Japanese school system, third graders in junior high school are about fifteen years old.

cannot vocalize smoothly, however hard he or she may try. Whenever he or she comes across those sounds, he or she will try to camouflage the stutter by rephrasing the word or adding another sound before the problematic one. For instance, if you have difficulty in articulating the word, '*yamanote-sen*,'[6] you can use its antiquated name, '*sho-sen*.'[7] Or, if you cannot easily utter '*chikatetsu*,'[8] you can use the English word 'subway' instead. Or, when you need to say '*Ueda-desu*,'[9] and you stutter when saying '*ue*,' you can make it a longer sentence, such as, '*Setagaya no Ueda-desu*,'[10] or '*Toyota Fudosan no Ueda-desu*.'[11]

In this way, a stutterer contrives various strategies in order not to stutter in conversation. Due to this skilful cover-up, those who have nothing to do with stuttering are easily deceived, and cannot tell a stutterer from a non-stutterer. However, in the case of proper nouns and place names, stutterers cannot use these devices. The simple task of calling out names and saying place names is the hardest task for a stutterer.

After the lecture, the headmaster of the cram school said apologetically, 'Mr. Araki, your English is good enough,

---

[6] *Yamanote-sen*: JR Yamanote line. It is a loop line in the central Tokyo.

[7] *Sho-sen*: an old name for the national railway. After 1949, it was called '*kokutetsu*,' literally meaning a national railway, before it was divided into several JR railway companies.

[8] *Chikatetsu*: underground.

[9] '*Ueda-desu*': 'This is Ueda'

[10] '*Setagaya no Ueda-desu*': 'This is Ueda from Setagaya.'

[11] '*Toyota Fudosan no Ueda-desu*': 'This is Ueda of Toyota Real Estate.'

but…. Well, if you have that kind of tendency in your speech, it is difficult to manage the lectures.' He was very careful in choosing his words, and I remember very clearly that I said, 'It was no good, was it?' to help him out. The headmaster said in a relieved way, 'I am sorry, but it is as you have said.' I stood up saying, 'I'm sorry,' then he asked, 'Mr. Araki, have you stuttered since you were small?' When I replied, 'yes,' he said, 'You had better fix it.' Then I said, 'I think so, too,' without looking at him and left.

Until that day, I did not know I could stutter so severely. Naturally, I knew I stuttered, but I thought I could manage somehow even when I did. On that sunny day in April, it was me who was the most surprised by the severity of my stuttering. I was more than surprised; I was utterly devastated. No, I was not even devastated for a while; I felt empty inside.

I was supposed to take an interview and exam at another cram school the next day, but I did not go. I stayed home and went through, one by one, all the humiliating experiences I had had in my childhood, when I stuttered and was laughed at or received unwanted sympathy. Externally, I do not think I looked any different from my usual self that day, though. When I went out to Shinjuku and met my friends at Fugetsudo, they even said to me, 'You're always so cheerful,' since I was joking the whole time. My reputation in Shinjuku among my mates generally was that of 'a guy without a care or a worry in the world.' I wrote 'generally,' because there were one or two who saw through to my suffering at the deepest part of my soul.

Intense Self-Loathing

I was walking on the street in Shinjuku, with my ugly self-image, my awkward stutter, filling my thoughts. I was filled with an intense self-loathing. As I was walking along, drowning in my self-loathing that was paradoxically both distressing and seductive, I realized why I could not love Angela fully. It was because I saw my ugly self reflected in Angela, who also stuttered.

Of course, this truth must have been obvious to me for a long time, probably since the first day I met Angela. When I saw Angela stutter, especially in public, it aroused a sense of inferiority and self-hatred in me, and I was humiliated and disgusted, as if I myself had stuttered. I thought somewhere in my mind that I could not love her deeply. I was also very aware, on the other hand, that Angela and I got along better than best friends, or even siblings.

And yet, in order for the romantic flame between a man and a woman to burn, you need a strong emotion like admiration, a dreamlike and peaceful state of mind that allows you to forget your own shortcomings, if only temporarily, when you are beside that person.

Looking back on my state of mind thus far, it dawns on me now why I was able to love Angela from the bottom of my heart while we were alone together in Kujukuri, and why my feelings toward Angela suddenly grew shaky when we returned to Tokyo. In our secluded seaside life, no matter how many times Angela stuttered, I was the only witness. Neither

Angela nor I was exposed to the '(cold) gaze of the other,' in the term favoured by the Existentialists. I was able to stay calm when there was no 'gaze of the other' around. But back in Tokyo, the situation changed drastically. Every time Angela stuttered, even slightly, the 'gaze of the other' that witnessed her stutter stung my heart. Even the slightest reaction in the 'gaze of the other' made me feel as if I myself had been caught stuttering, or rather, it made me more conscious of my own stuttering and tormented me inside with my own sense of inferiority.

For example, I remember I was ashamed when I saw Angela stutter while talking with my brother's wife. I also remember how I felt embarrassed and humiliated when John teased Angela about her stuttering, or when she stuttered in front of a British woman who then laughed reservedly, or when my mate looked a bit embarrassed at seeing Angela stutter. I was ashamed and humiliated more intensely than when I myself stuttered.

That April, when I was forced to face my own severe stuttering, I was also forced to face my true feelings for Angela.

Angela's Return to Japan

I looked for a job that did not require me to talk in public. There were many options if I was not too picky. In those days, the Japanese economy was booming. I slowly began walking into a new stage of my life. My daily activities, however, were not much different, as I would go to Shinjuku after work to meet friends, talk to girls, and write novels in a corner of a café.

What changed in me was my way of thinking, and this change showed clearly in my writing. I quit writing about fantastic antiheroes and heroic characters, and started writing about my juvenile experiences and my family. I began to think I should write on the issues that I had avoided looking at thus far, such as my origin, my essence, and my core self.

Around that time, I had several interesting jobs where I penned original stories for *manga*, and translated articles for a magazine targeting youth. Unfortunately, interesting jobs like these were scarce, and I mainly worked as a private English tutor and as a temporary manual worker.

Angela often wrote to me. She wrote that she was coming back to Japan in July. She also wrote that she had officially divorced her husband. I wrote affectionate letters to her in return, but my mind was in turmoil. There was a feeling growing inside me that made me hesitate, or refuse, to live with Angela again.

At the end of July when the rainy season ended and the crazy Japanese summer began, Angela came back.[12] Angela arrived at Yokohama Port, but I did not go to pick her up in Yokohama, as I was busy that day. I thought we would be able to meet eventually, if I was at Fugetsudo or some other place in Shinjuku. Then again, I could have also thought it was all right if we did not meet at all, hoping to avoid her.

One hot and humid day that summer, I met Angela in

---

[12] According to Gordon, it was 17 July, 1971 (p. 185).

Fugetsudo. From that day on, for four or five consecutive days, Angela and I spent what was a hard and painful time together. Part of me was happy to see Angela again, and enjoyed talking about the three months we were apart. However, what weighed on my mind heavily all the while was a feeling that, 'I have to make up my mind soon.' Sensing my gloominess, Angela was also nervous and irritated. On the second or third day after our reunion, I decided to break up with her. I felt as though I could not bear the sight of Angela anymore. Choosing the least acerbic words I could, I told her that we had better live separately.

Angela took my change of heart as betrayal. She accused me of being 'a liar' and 'an immature man thinking only of himself.' She even slapped my face once with all her might. Agreeing with Angela's accusation, I considered myself 'a liar,' 'a betrayer,' and 'an immature man thinking only of myself,' and I said so to her. Angela wanted to know what had happened during the three months she had been away from Japan, and asked me questions. I said nothing about my stuttering incident. After those five or so days together, we began to go our separate ways.

Angela's New Boyfriend

My memory is hazy, but Angela temporarily lived in an apartment in Meidai-mae[13] where only foreigners resided, and then moved to a ground floor flat in an old-ish house in Takadano-

---

[13] Meidai-mae: the area relatively close to both Shinjuku and Shibuya.

baba. I visited her once at the foreigners-only apartment, and two or three times at the house in Takadanobaba.

Though I do not remember what we were arguing about, when we were alone in her room at the house in Takadanobaba, I remember Angela started hitting me again. I let Angela hit me as many times as she wanted, and suddenly tears rolled down from my eyes. Seeing them, Angela said, 'Why are you crying? It's me who wants to cry.' When I said to her, 'It's a relief to cry,' Angela gave me a dumbfounded look and repeated, 'It's me who wants to cry.'

After that, I often came across Angela at Fugetsudo in Shinjuku or on the street. If both of us felt like it, we would go to another café and have a chat. After a while, I learned that Angela had a new boyfriend. According to her, he was a *Zainichi* Korean.[14] When she first told me about her new boyfriend, she said to me – 'You and I had nothing in common, when I come to think of it. Nothing at all. And your lifetime idol, Elvis? He's really lame.'

I was disappointed a little, thinking she was a commonplace woman after all, and asked her, 'Do you have many things in common with your new boyfriend, then?' To this, Angela replied, 'Yes, a lot.' I secretly wondered whether all women were like this, and felt the weight on my mind diminishing significantly.

There was one incident regarding Angela's new boyfriend.

---

[14] *Zainichi* Korean: Korean people living in Japan with special permanent resident status.

It was already winter, I believe. One evening, I went into Fugetsudo on my own and found 'honest' John sitting near the entrance. When I talked to him, he cheerfully said hello, but cast nervous sidelong glances toward the back of the café. His behaviour was so odd it made me look in the same direction, where I found Angela talking with other white people. This discovery in itself was nothing special, but I saw a young Asian man standing right beside Angela. 'I see, he's the reason why John is nervous,' I thought, and said to John, 'See you,' and left Fugetsudo at once, pretending not to notice anything, because I did not want to make him worry too much.

As I left Fugetsudo, I thought, 'A funny guy, that John is. There's nothing to worry about.' But then, a certain memory came back to me, and a suspicion flashed across my mind. It was two or three months after we separated; we were talking on the street in Shinjuku, and Angela said to me, 'Everybody thinks that you left me, but the truth is that I left you. I was so fed up with you.' As I remembered her words, I thought, 'Angela must have told John and the others that she left me. That's why John was so nervous to see me. He must have worried that if I saw Angela and her new boyfriend together, I might become furious and fly out at them or something.'

To protect her own womanly happiness and pride, she did not hesitate to reverse the facts in her mind. Many women are similarly ingenious. We men are tormented all our lives by these lies, so simple and yet so obvious – lies peculiar to womankind. I was a bit disappointed because another one of the good images I had of Angela was shattered at that moment.

I had believed that Angela was a more radical realist and was free from womanly weakness and opportunism.

Angela and I continued to bump into each other in the city or in cafés, even after this silly incident. Sometimes she appeared in Fugetsudo late at night with a face like a ghost, as if she had been drained of all her energy. She must have spent days absorbed in writing a novel or something similar.

Angela's Gradual Change

Whenever I saw her from time to time, I noticed that Angela was gradually changing. Once, when she was talking to me about her foreign friends as usual, I said to her cynically, 'Why are you staying in Japan? If you're only interested in Caucasians, you should go back to England as soon as possible. I'm sure more white people live in England than in Tokyo.' She retorted, 'There are many interesting Japanese people. But all the Japanese men I'm interested in can't speak English.' When I said, 'Then you need to learn Japanese,' Angela said, 'It would take at least ten years for me to speak reasonably well.' Angela had never said such a thing when she was living with me.

I also often saw her with Japanese women. One of the Japanese women she was with turned out to be a lesbian. A female friend of the woman said, 'I introduced her to Angela, thinking she might also be a lesbian.' But I could not detect a lesbian aura from Angela at all. That kind of thing had never happened before, either.

Once, when I was talking about a novel I had written, Angela became very curious, and suggested, 'Why don't you translate it into English? I can pay you a little translation fee. I want to know what kind of stories you write.' I was enthusiastic about her suggestion, and thought of translating my writing. For reasons I do not recall now, the project did not proceed any further and evaporated.

I sometimes wondered what Angela and I had been doing, and why the things that I have written about here happened between us in the stretch of a year and several months. To these questions, one man, a friend of mine who was also close to Angela, offered a concise answer. His words made me so happy and content that I still remember them well. He told me that when he had met Angela, she said, 'I loved Sozo desperately.' I do not understand at all why she loved me so 'desperately,' but I am sure her emotions were the source of everything that happened between the two of us.

I do not have any more memories of Angela after that. I probably never saw Angela again. After a while, about half a year after I stopped seeing Angela, I received a letter from Angela via my brother. At that time, I was living with a Japanese woman in Asagaya.[15] It was a letter filled with nostalgia and humour unique to Angela. I do not remember the contents of the letter, apart from the fact that it was overflowing with friendship and affection. I wanted to write her back, but not knowing what to write, I kept on postponing. Before long,

---

[15] Asagaya: the fifth stop from Shinjuku on the JR Chuo line (west of Shinjuku).

Angela's letter was lost.

Two years later, I opened an English cram school myself and began teaching English. I taught various students, from elementary school pupils to high school students preparing for college examinations, as well as housewives, and working adults. My stuttering had not been cured, but it was better than in the days when I was living with Angela. I often stuttered, but was able to manage the class and the number of students increased. I was beginning to accept myself as a stutterer. I no longer hated myself as before, even when I stuttered. It probably meant that I had grown up a little.

As a writer, I wrote essays and translated articles for a magazine targeting youth every month. My racism, which used to be intense, had mostly disappeared before I knew it, and I had come to befriend some white people in Tokyo in a much more relaxed way than before. I still felt a strong ideological resistance in accepting the values of Caucasian society, and I was not pleased to see Japanese people flatter Caucasian people. I did not become furious at them anymore, though.

I still did not make much of, or like, Japanese society and culture. Despite whether I liked it or not, I came to regard the whole thing as trivial. In other words, I became able to distance myself from them and see them objectively.

I reminisced about Angela quite often, and thought, 'If I had been what I am now, I would not have needed to break up with her, and could have lived with her without any problem.' I even thought, 'A stuttering couple would be charming.' I realized then how unbelievably immature I was when I was with Angela, and my heart was often wrung with such shame and remorse that I would bend my back and groan out loud.

I was planning to go to London sooner or later to see Angela. I wanted to meet her and talk about various things and argue with her, like we used to. I imagined that if Angela heard about my new way of thinking, she might be pleased or scornful as before, and I would become angry at her or she would become angry at me, and in this way, we would be able to have a good time. I thought I would be able to obtain her address by inquiring at a newsagent or such, and I believed we could meet at any time.

Fifteen years later, I learned from a newspaper article that Angela had died of cancer. Learning that she had married again, to a younger man, and had had a child, I fondly imagined her having a happy life, and pictured her peaceful smile in my mind.

From around that time, I myself began publishing prolifically, though it had little to do with literature and was on the topic of psychology. Incidentally, I later married the woman I had been living with in Asagaya. During the first two or three years of cohabitation with this woman, I felt stronger cultural differences than I did with Angela. Culturally and habitually, this woman felt much more alien to me. When I met her parents for the first time, I literally felt as if I had become Alice in *Alice in Wonderland*. Even setting aside the fact that we shared the same stuttering disorder, I still think Angela and I were very similar.

Epilogue: Angela Carter, Myself, and My Monster

It was more than four decades ago, in 1969, when I first met Angela. When I look back and remember who I was then, I am filled with remorse rather than sweet memories. Come to think of it, what had initially drawn me to Angela and what eventually made me feel repelled by her was the same monster in my heart – a monstrous 'inferiority complex' – by which I was helplessly controlled and consumed back in those days. I suppose such a monster resides in the shadows of each and every one of our hearts, and none can escape it; every heart is more or less eaten up by this monster. It is probable that both Angela and I secretly kept the same monster in our chests, and struggled with it in the same way. Because of this, I felt close to her, as if she were my sister, and we were able to open up and talk about anything and everything. But, in the end, this similarity made her seem repulsive to me. I came to feel that she was forcing me to see what I did not desire to see. Perhaps it only shows that the grip of the monster was tighter on me than on her.

When one's heart is eaten away by this monster called an 'inferiority complex,' one's own sensibilities and thoughts become twisted, and one feels acute pain and anguish coming from one's battered heart. It may seem surprising, but this wound to one's mind, more often than not, is unfortunately inflicted when one is very young. If this unfortunate situation continues, one's behaviour grows destructive and erratic. At a very young age, this destructive and erratic behaviour is mostly introverted, and therefore it is not noticeable from the outside. But as one grows older, it gradually stands out. In extreme cases, it manifests in suicide attempts or criminal activities, like homicide.

An 'inferiority complex,' in my opinion, is different in nature from the temporary sense of inferiority that one inescapably feels during the race for survival that is life. Sure enough, those who experience difficulties during this survival race, such as, say, students who always get low grades in school, may feel disappointed and as if they have failed. However, rarely are their hearts wounded so deeply as to become suicidal or to make them want to kill other students who achieved better grades. Most of the time, they simply learn their own limitations, and that encourages them to find their strength in some other field. They survive the experience of temporary failure, and they, in their own manner and time, return to the race sooner or later.

To me, an 'inferiority complex' does not seem to be rooted in such a simple experience of failure or temporary inferiority, but in a much more subtle and private emotional flux. In fact, inferiority complexes have not yet been fully explained by modern psychology. I am certain that they are connected to a desire we all have from our infancy: the desire to be loved and liked, which is often left unfulfilled.

It is important to note, in order to be loved and liked, how one needs to be charming in a certain way, even at a very young age. It seems to me that, as society grows richer and the education level of the population rises, society's preference for charming kids intensifies, and the charmless child is left unloved. The tendency is certainly very strong in modern Japan, where the relationship between parents and children is like one between friends, and children are often treated like spoiled pets.

Unloved, unappreciated children struggle in the face of their unreasonable fate without really knowing why they are not cared for or loved. They may become cranky in order to gain attention or, sometimes, they may try destructive behaviour, to no avail. They may eventually notice that they lack some quality. (It may be more fortunate for them if they do not notice.)

When they do notice their lack, often they dig deep into the nature of it, even though they are hurting inside. In doing so, the childish imagination plays a significant role, as they build layers of imagined reasons to explain their own charmlessness. In the end, a simple, insignificant shortcoming becomes a giant, complicated, insurmountable obstacle. A large portion of it has no objectivity, and in fact, it is often a product of pure imagination. In this way, an inferiority complex is brought into existence.

Those children caught in the web of an inferiority complex try their best not to look at the thing that tortures them. They avoid looking into themselves, their true selves, by fleeing into the delusory 'charming' selves they create in their imaginations. The stronger their inferiority complexes are, the more powerful this delusion becomes.

Sometimes, the delusory self does not remain a delusion. It propels children to start doing various activities. Some try their best academically at school, some at sports, some at having fun, some at doing what they are not supposed to be doing, such as vandalism or fighting, some at superficially copying someone with obvious charm, some at various forms of art, such as literature, music, etc.

Quite a few children suffering from inferiority complexes become involved in artistic activities. I think it is because art itself is directly related to charm. Through artistic activities, one acknowledges one's strength and demonstrates it by using individuality as a tool.

Relationships are – or rather, romantic love itself is – also an effort toward self-salvation in order to obtain a 'lovable' self.

Through various activities such as these, children with inferiority complexes attempt to heal their wounds and fabricate 'lovable' selves. Their way of life, consumed by such efforts, does not change during puberty, adolescence, or until well into adulthood. No, I should say, rather, their pursuit of a 'lovable self' becomes more vigorous and pragmatic as they grow older. In an attempt to establish their individuality, they try to create a unique way of expressing themselves, and pour enormous energy into silly love games. Of course, all of these are done in an effort to construct their 'lovable selves.'

When Angela Carter and I met some forty years ago, both of us were, I think, in the process described above. In stark contrast to Angela, however, who was talented and already established as a writer, I myself was only a foolish youngster who had not accomplished a single thing. It was only in my mid-forties that I became able to make ends meet by writing, I am sorry to say.

Perhaps because both of us were trapped in the same inferiority complex, Angela Carter and I were, in my opinion, very similar. We were like brother and sister, or cousins who had grown up in the same environment. I cherish all the memories of the time in my life that I shared with her, but especially precious are the memories of how we debated, discussed, made jokes and ironic commentaries, and how we had good laughs together. On such occasions, both Angela and I were able to freely express not only ourselves, but also our affection toward each other, because, I think, we did not have to worry about our inferiority complexes, nesting within the deep shadows of our hearts.

Since breaking up with her, and occasionally receiving her letters from England, I had wanted to go to London to visit her again, debate with her, have witty conversations with her, joke with her, and have a good laugh together. Of course, I felt bad about leaving her, but it never occurred to me that I should apologize. I did not think that Angela would appreciate it at all even if I did.

I learned of Angela's death from a newspaper article. I was shocked, as I never imagined she would die so young. I was also surprised to know she had been married again and had a child. It was impossible to imagine the young Angela I knew as a happily married wife. At the same time, thinking, 'Angela must have found ordinary happiness' made me happy. I vividly remember a sarcastic, unpleasant thought also surfacing in my mind: 'a premature death by cancer must have been a good thing for her, because it put an end to her long suffering.' However, the strongest emotion that filled me then was loneliness – the feeling that I could never see Angela again and talk to her, debate with her, or make sarcastic comments together.

When it was suggested that I should write about the time I spent with Angela Carter, I thought of writing it in the form of a novel at first. However, as I was playing with the idea in my mind for a couple of days, it gradually dawned on me that it was better to write what had occurred in a direct and truthful manner, and I made up my mind to do so.

What I tried to accomplish in this memoir was to write what I remembered as truthfully as I could, to avoid whitewashing or inserting lofty interpretations. I tried to return to myself forty years ago, when I was twenty-five, to recollect what I had thought and felt, then and to record it as truthfully as possible, referring as little as possible to my current thoughts or feelings. I also tried to write everything fairly, whether it was good or bad, meaningful or meaningless, fun or bitter, no matter how much I felt proud or ashamed of it. The reason is that I now reckon this memoir could never serve as some kind of advocacy or lesson, nor as some plea. The purpose of my writing, as I understand now, is to tell readers about one relationship, a romantic relationship that lived and died in Japan forty-some years ago, as truthfully as it existed (even though that may in fact be impossible). I think it may be interesting to today's British readers to know how a Japanese youngster saw, and felt about, British or American people forty years ago. Also, it may be of certain value to today's Japanese youth to learn what a young person in Tokyo forty years ago had in mind, and what kind of life he led. Most of all, it may be of great significance to the fans and researchers of Angela Carter, the novelist, to have a peek into a chapter of her life, no matter how brief it was.

Sozo Araki

Her Side of the Story (Afterword by the Translator)[1]

Natsumi Ikoma

Japan was a society in flux in 1969, when Angela Carter came for what was originally planned to be a short visit. By then, Japan was no longer the sad, depressed, deflated nation that was defeated in World War II. And yet, it had not become the economic giant that it later became known as. The population was growing, the cities expanding, the infrastructure developing – though the super-modernity and urbanity that Japan is famous for today were still not in sight. People were looking ahead to a potentially bright and powerful future, though they were also suffering from an intense inferiority complex in the knowledge that their society was still lagging behind the great Europe and the even greater United States, whose civilisation infiltrated Japanese people's daily lives through imported hardware as well as TV programs, films, and music. The Japanese people were no longer Oriental savages (though I am not sure if we ever were), but modernised creatures so Westernised as to have no sense of belonging to Asia, let alone the Orient, a somewhat romanticised notion created by the Occidentals.

In such a historical moment, Angela Carter came to Japan on her own without her husband by her side and met Sozo Araki – fell in love with him. He was six years younger than she was and aspiring to be a writer, whereas Angela was already established. Sozo Araki himself embodied those changes that were taking place in Japan in the seventies, inferiority complex and all, though Angela was initially unaware of it. She was still married to Paul Carter, but was contemplating leaving him while in the throes of indecision.

Angela and Sozo's love affair was intense. It persisted for about two years until the summer of 1971, interspersed with Angela's short visits back to England. They lived together, and travelled to many places. It may have been just two years of Angela's life, but the relationship created a huge impact on her literary style, choice of motifs, and her sense of self. Cultural as well as psychological observations she made during her time with Sozo contributed immensely to expanding her literary universe and sharpening her understanding of the complicated world of human beings. It was not just an encounter with the new and the exotic; it was infinitely more complex than that. Love and desire were ensnared between wars of cultural, racial, and sexual dominance, patriarchal control, and personal psychological problems, in which the unfamiliar and the familiar intermingled. Angela's relationship with Sozo changed her. Through it, she learned so much about him and about Japanese men, about human beings in general, and above all, about herself.

It is no longer possible to know how Angela Carter might have reacted upon reading Sozo's memoir and his confession as to the true reasons behind their break-up. Though informative, Sozo's memoir is only half of the story – his side of the story – nothing more, nothing less. After all, it is a reconstruction after many decades; the memories may have been altered, organized themselves in ways different from actuality. His male chauvinism might have affected his narrative and his interpretation of the events that transpired. In addition to all of this, to begin with, the communication between the couple was not fully functional because of the language difference, which inevitably led to misunderstandings. Therefore, after reading what Sozo wrote, I became all the more intrigued to find out what Angela herself had recorded about Sozo and her relationship with him – to know her side of the story.

In an attempt at uncovering Angela's view on their relationship, I made several trips to the British Library, where the journals and letters of Angela Carter are archived. There I found, in her journals, that Angela not only mentioned Sozo Araki repeatedly, but rather minutely recorded what occurred between them. She also wrote down titles and excerpts of the books and poetry she had read, ideas for her stories, and often drawings she had sketched. The entries are mostly undated, therefore it is difficult to separate the record of what actually happened to Angela from her literary, fictional writings. Sometimes they seem inseparably intertwined.

Some are, however, quite obviously about Sozo, those of which I made copies of in my own research notebooks. Unfortunately, reproduction of those journal entries is not permitted, so I cannot share them here. I strongly believe her side of the story must be heard and it should be in her own words, but, with the hopeless realisation that my attempt to complement Sozo's one-sided memoir and to attain the whole picture is, from the outset, a doomed one, I, nonetheless, will hereby try to create a narrative that is not so one-sided with whatever sources I can use, including the invaluable biography written by Edmund Gordon. Still, what we can obtain at best would be a partial peek at a relationship that has been irredeemably lost. But, I hope it may nevertheless help increase our understanding of Angela Carter's literary universe better.

Sozo in Angela Carter's Journal

Sozo's name first appears in one of Angela's journal entries written presumably in 1969. It is the very first blueprint of the short story, 'A Souvenir of Japan,' and Sozo's name is written beside the title, though the name is crossed out with a black line. From this story, we learn that Angela's attraction to Sozo is largely physical when she writes that she finds him 'incredibly beautiful' (qtd. in Gordon 140). She likens him to art objects, animals, and mythic figures, and describes his Asian beauty in great detail, showing that initially, her attraction to Sozo might have been tinged with Orientalist fantasy.

It seems that shortly after she met Sozo for the first time, Angela created this blueprint of the story, which she later developed into the version we now know. Considering that it was drafted just after Angela first met Sozo, we can see what a strong impression Sozo made on her. In the final product, Carter describes the 'love hotel' Sozo took her to their first night, and how their love-making was repeatedly interrupted by a hotel maid who carried them a tea tray and towels. The

Her Side of the Story (Afterword by the Translator) 157

narrator of the story describes the Japanese lover as 'elegant' and 'androgynous,' and how his 'high cheekbones gave to his face the aspect of a mask.' She writes:

> His hair was so heavy his neck drooped under its weight and was of a black so deep it turned purple in sunlight. His mouth also was purplish and his blunt, bee-stung lips those of Gauguin's Tahitians. (*Fireworks* 6)

I found sentences very similar to these in her journal. From this initial entry onwards, many more references to Sozo fill the ensuing pages. At the beginning, her description of Sozo is tinged with delight in encountering the new and the exotic, though strangely familiar at the same time. His familiarity is what Angela stresses here: that he looks like someone she knew from her childhood, or someone from her fantasy. Looking back on the early days, she later wrote:

> His face did not, when I first met him, seem to me the face of a stranger; it seemed a face long known & well remembered, a face that had always been somehow imminent in my consciousness as an idea that now found a perfect visual expression... plainly, he was an object created in the mode of fantasy; his image was already present somewhere in my head, & I was seeking to discover him in reality, searching every face for the right face – that is, the face that corresponded to my notions of the imagined face of the one I should love. (qtd. in

Gordon 141)

Her words are intensely romantic in her description of how they were filled with passion on a freezing platform in Tokyo, waiting for the last train that would take them to his room. From Gordon's biography, we learn that Angela herself called the relationship with Sozo, 'my First Real Affair' (141). In a letter to a friend, Angela describes Sozo as 'a romantic of the most extreme kind…[he] possesses extreme charm, an intellect all the more remarkable because it is absolutely analytic & incapable of any kind of synthesis, and a relentless conviction of the utter futility of everything' (qtd. in Gordon 141). She found him charming and attractive, though she was also a level-headed analyst at the same time, finding from early on a touch of pessimism, male narcissism, repressed masochism, and neuroticism in him.

After the description of their initial infatuation period, which lasted only a little less than a fortnight, her journal records things that happened during her 6 months' return to England. According to Gordon's biography, Angela had made up her mind by the time she left Japan to divorce her husband, Paul, and to return to Japan. She notified her intention in letters to Paul and friends. She wrote in her letters to friends, 'I fell in love & realised that Paul is a selfish pig, lousy in bed & shockingly insensitive' and 'I can't live with him any more or I'll kill myself' (qtd. in Gordon 142). She quite savagely cut Paul out from her life. Then her mother, with whom she had a complicated relationship, died. Angela's mother had been displeased about her daughter's divorce from Paul, and died without resolving their conflict, leaving Angela shattered. During this difficult period, the thought of going back to Sozo seemed to have been Angela's emotional anchor.

On 19 April 1970, Angela returned to Japan with the intention of delving more deeply into Japanese life – life with Sozo. Her journal entries about him become more passionate and self-reflective, often with descriptions of sex, too, though not in a sensational or provocative way, but with a pensive and analytical tone. When they go to a hotel straight from the airport upon her arrival, she writes, 'sustained by passion only, we walk the tightrope of desire and acrobatically peform the double somersault of love without a safety net' (qtd. in Gordon 153). As Gordon points out, many versions of this sentence appear in her later writings, such as 'A Souvernir of Japan,' 'Flesh and the Mirror,' *The Infernal Desire Machines of Doctor Hoffman* and *Nights at the Circus*, connecting the idea of performance and desire, an important literary motif in Angela's later works.

She describes Araki's physique often from a connoisseur's point of view, praising his physical beauty using many aesthetic terms. For instance, in 'A Souvenir of Japan,' she writes, 'I should have liked to have had him embalmed and been able to keep him beside me in a glass coffin, so that I could watch him all the time' (*Fireworks* 6). But things did not stay so rosy all the time once they started living together in a residential area in Meguro. Conflict began to surface. One of the issues was Sozo's financial dependence on Angela. The expensive rent meant the majority had to be covered by Angela, because she earned significantly more than Sozo. Another was his unrealized dream of becoming a writer. Obviously, it must have hurt Sozo's male ego that he had to depend on Angela, who was a successful writer, when his future as a writer was nowhere to be seen. Still, she was besotted, feeling his magic spell upon herself, but she gradually came to realize that her fantasy might not have been the same as reality when she discovered Sozo's neuroticism and various complexes were darker than she had thought.

Very importantly, Angela wrote in one journal entry affectionately about Sozo's stuttering – how he stuttered when he spoke in Japanese. From this single mention of stuttering, we cannot deduce how stuttering affected Angela psychologically. If Sozo's guess is correct, and I feel it might be, this brief entry proves that she denied the impact stuttering had on herself, though in her subconscious it played a significant part, hence she was touched by Sozo's stutter. We can only surmise that stuttering was indeed what connected Angela and Sozo on a subconscious level. With or without this common affliction, Angela felt, 'he is exactly like me' (qtd. in Gordon 156), even going as far to say that 'I knew him as intimately as I knew my own image in a mirror' (*Fireworks* 8).

After this are entries with Sozo's name as the title in several instalments, scattered across the subsequent pages. Described here are her anxieties about the state the couple was in: his contradictory behaviour, passionate kisses and then not coming

Her Side of the Story (Afterword by the Translator) 161

home for many consecutive nights, how she was affected by this turbulence. She realised they were so co-dependent now that they could not live without each other, but at the same time, the other's presence was so stifling that in each other's company, they would die from the lack of freedom. Amidst this turmoil, though sex with Sozo was still so good, Angela wrote about her decision to eventually break up with him – a decision she never carried out herself. She found herself in a hopeless dead-end she could not escape from because she loved Sozo so much, even though she knew his unreliable behaviour would never make her happy. In a letter to her friend, she writes:

> I am both absolutely in love with him, so that he seems the only real thing in the world, and irritated beyond measure by his unpunctuality, his vagueness, his (yes) absent-mindedness and curious capacity for seeming to be lying when he is, in fact, telling the truth. (qtd. in Gordon 156)

This state of conflict, from my perspective, did tremendous good to Angela Carter's literature, since she started to analyse her own mind as well as her relationship with Sozo with more objectivity and self-reflection, as though her own mind were a stranger to her. She did independent research on Japanese culture, society and history, and it seems she read many books related to Japan. She was obviously interested in why she was attracted to Sozo so illogically, and set out to find the reason.

She also analysed the psychology of being in love, of being in a romantic relationship and in a power-game between genders, and the mental state love creates in human beings. Angela used her analytical findings in many of her later works, including stories in *Fireworks* and *The Bloody Chamber*, essays collected in *Shaking a Leg*, and novels like *The Infernal Desire Machines of Doctor Hoffman* and *The Passion of New Eve*.

In her journal, Carter also writes a plan for a new novel that would later become *The Infernal Desire Machines of Doctor Hoffman* (1972). She writes an extensive description of the beautiful seaside village of Katakai Beach, located in the Kujukuri area of Chiba prefecture – the very same village Sozo spent many pages in his memoir describing as the setting of his most treasured memories with Angela. It was in this village that Angela wrote *The Infernal Desire Machines of Doctor Hoffman*, the widely-acclaimed novel she herself reckoned as her major achievement. The heroine, Albertina, is modelled after Sozo, as attested by Angela herself in a letter to a friend. When she was writing the novel in Chiba, their relationship was peaceful and happy, but the novel's tragic and ironic ending, in which the power struggle between the two cannot help but obliterate one or the other and lead them to ultimate disillusionment, foretold the direction in which their relationship was heading. Though Carter was tormented in finding repeated evidence of Sozo's infidelity and inconsistency, and in spite of moments of feminist anger toward his chauvinistic attitude, of her craving for independence, and of detachment from it all, she stayed in the relationship.

According to Gordon, Angela left for England after finishing writing the larger part of *Hoffman* to attend to practical matters, like finalising the divorce with Paul and applying for a re-entry visa. When she came back to Japan on 17 July 1971, Sozo was not there to greet her. What happened then was turned into the story, 'Flesh and the Mirror.' She apparently went to Shinjuku and walked around street after street in search of Sozo, and ended up having a one-night stand with a stranger. The next morning, she tracked down Sozo at Fugetsudo and they had a massive row, but the true reason behind his detachment was unknown to her. She wrote, 'He is undergoing some sort of personality crisis which I don't quite understand ... I think he himself has just realised he's not a student but a dropout & this has come as something of a shock' (qtd. in Gordon 188). Before long, the hidden issues and conflicts between them all came erupting out. She wrote in a letter to her friend, 'He says I have dominated him completely,' 'a simpler & less competitive person [than Sozo] might be moved by the fact that I couldn't have written HOFFMAN without him ... This is how a good wife should feel. Well, he reacted violently against the wife role' (qtd. in Gordon 188-189). They continued arguing for several days, at the end of which they broke up.

In the last journal instalment with 'Sozo' as a title, Sozo is only mentioned in the past tense. Angela describes the state of devastation she was in, and how they had devoured each other like enemies, all the while clinging to each other like drowning lovers. After that is a long excerpt from a poem, the fifth part from 'Extracts from Addresses to the Academy of Fine Ideas,' written by Wallace Stevens. Angela's side-note suggests it was meant as an epitaph for Sozo:

v
The law of chaos is the law of ideas,
Of improvisations and seasons of belief.

Ideas are men. The mass of meaning and
The mass of men are one. Chaos is not

The mass of meaning. It is three or four
Ideas or, say, five men or, possibly six.

In the end, these philosophic assassins pull
Revolvers and shoot each other. One remains.

The mass of meaning becomes composed again.
He that remains plays on an instrument

A good agreement between himself and night,
A chord between the mass of men and himself,

Far, far beyond the putative canzones
Of love and summer. The assassin sings

> In chaos and his song is a consolation.
> It is the music of the mass of meaning.
>
> And yet it is a singular romance,
> This warmth in the blood-world for the pure idea,
>
> This inability to find a sound,
> That clings to the minds like that right sound, that song
>
> Of the assassin that remains and sings
> In the high imagination, triumphantly. (255-256)

It appears that around the time of their break-up, she wrote this section in her journal. From this quotation, we can at least fathom that Angela saw in the end Sozo and she (both of them with their own ideas and ideologies) had been trying to assassinate each other, and that they had no hope ahead of them in their destructive relationship. We cannot know whether it was her or him who really initiated the break-up, but the bitter and sad entries in Angela's journal suggest she did not want to be parted from Sozo just yet. After this excerpt, Angela wrote a long reflection upon her now broken relationship with Sozo. The pain Carter went through in trying to come to terms with the break-up with Sozo and to make sense of her relationship with him is tangible in those sentences. Scarred by what had transpired, a few days later she wrote the title for her new story with the same word used by Wallace Stevens, 'assassin,' suggesting it is about Sozo. She also used the same word in describing the relationship between Albertina and Desiderio in *Hoffman*, making it all the more suitable an elegy for her own relationship with Sozo.

The rest of the journal is about post-Sozo life in Japan and about a new boyfriend, a Korean-Japanese teenage boy younger than Sozo. Mentions of Sozo become short, scarce, dry, cynical, and generally more distant, although the amount Carter wrote about Sozo is far more than the amount she wrote about the Korean boyfriend. In one entry, she even adds a comical note two years later, laughing that she did not recognise the person she had been. It lets us get a glimpse at Angela Carter with new insights and new perspectives, strengthened by her past experiences. In another entry, she contemplates leaving Japan and leaving the Korean boyfriend behind, and seems to be surprised by the fact that she can do it more easily than when she was with Sozo. From the journal, we know Angela continued seeing Sozo from time to time as a friend, until she finally left Japan. It is on a new notebook Carter records how she left Japan and started a new life, a new self, a new adventure.

Sozo's Shadow in the Works of Angela Carter

As I mentioned, and as Angela herself noted, *The Infernal Desire Machines of Doctor Hoffman* (1972) owes much to Angela's analysis of her own romantic relationship with Sozo, and to her conclusion that lovers inevitably become each other's assassin.[2] Albertina in this work is modelled after Sozo, but the novel is more fundamentally influenced by Sozo himself and Angela's relationship with him, because her analysis of romantic relationships in this novel could have only been attained from experiencing the mutually devouring relationship Angela had with Sozo. The protagonist of the novel, Desiderio – named after desire – was initially attracted to Albertina's otherness, but in the end, after experiencing many ordeals with her, he finds her boringly similar to himself, which propels him to kill her contradictorily to save his romance. Perhaps that was how Carter felt about Sozo at the end of their relationship.

Besides the obvious ones such as Taro in 'A Souvenir of Japan' and the assassin X in 'Elegy for a Freelance,' many characters in Angela Carter's stories included in the collection *Fireworks* – interestingly, many of whom are androgynous – are in fact at least partially modelled after Sozo. The two stories I just referred to are the first and the last in the collection, suggesting the special significance they had for Angela. We can even say that *Fireworks* is a fictionalised version of her journal entries during her Japan days. When she first met Sozo, she wrote the blueprint of 'A Souvenir of Japan.' When she separated from him, she copied the poetry by Wallace Stevens, which includes the word 'assassin,' and then marked it down as the title of her new story about Sozo. She sandwiched the rest of the stories between these two pieces containing Sozo characters, showing us how Sozo, or rather what Angela experienced in her relationship with him, dominated

Angela Carter's literary imagination related to Japan.

Indeed, what was crucial to Angela's imagination may not have been the actual human being called Sozo Araki, but the experience of being in a romantic relationship with a Japanese man in Japan then as a woman. Living among Japanese women who were treated as lesser citizens, sexual objects, or desexualised wives in the seventies, Angela found herself treated as an exception, an exotified object, but contradictorily (or not), also as less than a human being. Being in love in this situation was tricky business, because it made it more difficult to retain one's agency. In 'A Souvenir of Japan,' Angela writes:

> I had never been so absolutely the mysterious other. I had become a kind of phoenix, a fabulous beast; I was an outlandish jewel. He found me, I think, inexpressibly exotic. But I often felt like a female impersonator. (*Fireworks* 7)

As I have written elsewhere previously, Angela's awareness of gender in this quotation needs to be stressed:

> It is noteworthy that she writes 'a female impersonator' here, to signpost the narrating woman's awareness of the gendered expectations imposed upon her, and of the difference between what was desired and what she herself felt she was. Similarly, although on the surface Carter was adored and respected, she was able to penetrate that façade to see how Japanese society robbed her of her

subjectivity and agency. Instead, she was turned into an
object: a beast, a jewel, an automaton. (Ikoma 81)

Angela learned about extreme male-centrality in Japanese society in and outside of her relationship with Sozo, for instance when she worked as temporary staff at a hostess bar in the posh Ginza district in Tokyo among other foreign hostesses, who were deemed as a special attraction for male customers. After this experience, she wrote in an essay, 'Poor Butterfly,' '[T]he salesman explained: "a masturbatory device for gentlemen." Which is, presumably, the same function Suzy and I had performed for the last two and a half hours' (*Shaking a Leg* 254). She also realised this objectification of woman was not peculiar to Japanese society, but universally found in any patriarchal society when she wrote, '[T]he hostess – the computerized playmate – may conceivably be an illustration of the fact that Japan is just the same as everywhere else, only more so; perhaps she is indeed the universal male notion of the perfect woman' (251). The realisation of this universal notion of the 'perfect woman' must have been the driving force behind Carter's writing the widely acclaimed *The Internal Desire Machines of Doctor Hoffman* and the reason why she wrote, 'In Japan, I learnt what it is to be a woman, and became radicalised' (*Nothing Sacred* 28).

Angela connected sadism and masochism to typically Japanese personality traits. And in a romantic relationship in Japan, these traits are exhibited most intensely. For example, the narrator of 'A Souvenir of Japan' tells us how she and

Taro 'fought a silent battle of self-abnegation' (*Fireworks* 3). Angela surmised that romantic love in Japan inevitably forces masochism onto the ones involved. She writes in 'People as Pictures':

> [P]erhaps a repressive culture can only be maintained by a strong masochistic element among the repressed. ... More Japanese die of apoplexy than from anything else, as though they have bottled up their passions and bottled them up and bottled them up... until one day they just explode. (*Shaking a Leg* 238)

But the most important factor contributing to her hard-edged analyses, in my opinion, is the fact that Angela was in love. The short story, 'Flesh and the Mirror,' is a story that greatly resembles what Angela actually experienced in her relationship with Sozo, and in it she seems to be referring to what Judith Butler calls 'a sedimentation of gender norms' (Butler 524), which exerts its maximum force in the framework of romantic love. In 'Flesh and the Mirror,' she writes extensively about the risk involved in romantic love. It is the risk of losing oneself within the powerful ideology and narrative of romance. The narrator of 'Flesh and the Mirror' says:

> In order to create the loved object in this way and to issue it with its certificate of authentication, as beloved, I had also to labour at the idea of myself in love. I watched myself closely for all the signs and, precisely upon cue,

here they were! Longing, desire, self-abnegation, etc. ... I no longer understood the logic of my own performance. My script had been scrambled behind my back. The cameraman was drunk. The director had a *crise de nerfs* and been taken away to a sanatorium. (*Fireworks* 68)

Here, the narrator tells us how the ideology of romantic love strongly dictates her movement, how she has been consumed by masochism and loses her agency. She becomes a puppet manipulated by the puppet master. As I have written in a previously published paper, this shows 'how coercive romantic ideology, heterosexism and gender norms take away the agency of both parties in a romantic relationship' and that people in this society 'are persuaded, educated and coerced to plunge into heterosexual relationships. The script of romance they believe they have written themselves is in fact written by society and its ideology' (Ikoma 85).

Thus, the narrator of this story ends up becoming a performer of a script she does not recognise. The loss of agency in a romantic relationship and mutual assassination – the reader of this section may easily see the parallels with the relationship between Angela and Sozo. Carter herself experienced masochistic love with Sozo first-hand, and bottled up her passions in intense self-abnegation to the extent that she became a puppet, a self-less doll, until she and Sozo both became each other's assassin. I believe it is safe to say that the motifs of puppetry, performance, and assassination in Angela Carter's later works are immensely influenced by her romantic involvement with Sozo.

Angela gave an interview sometime in 1971 or 1972 about her experiences in Japan. Asked about her feelings for Japanese men, she answered:

> They're very beautiful! The young men, the Shinjuku people, have this very pure kind of dandyism that isn't a matter of clothes but has evolved into a method of presenting themselves to the world. When they grow their hair long they look like the best kind of Red Indian, and nature often blesses them with very impressive cheekbones and passionately sensitive mouths. And they move very beautifully. Yes, indeed. So a good deal of my pleasure has been aesthetic, really. I always like people to be beautiful. It seems the very least one can do. (Bell 26-27)

Then Carter refered more directly to her relationship with Sozo:

> Then, I lived with a Japanese national for a year. It is a great adventure to love a Japanese; much more so, maybe, than any of the other cross-cultural, cross-racial explorations, because of the peculiar severity of the Japanese idea of themselves. And one never knows where it will end because one becomes very much aware of the limitations of one's own culture as one – well, at any rate, I – learned more and more about the sheer

horror of being Japanese, of being a Japanese man, of the Procrustean bed of the traditional mores. But I was very happy most of the time, though it was always a complicated, feverish kind of happiness, because it was the kind of savage excitement an explorer feels in virgin land. There was a dreadful confusion of expectations, and I never knew what was going to happen next, because of the confusion. It was both an enriching and a devastating experience, and in many ways it was an affair with Japan itself. I went in the deep end and chose somebody who embodied much of the tensions of the country. And it is both enriching and devastating for a foreigner to live here, because of the confusion. (Bell 27)

I am certain the reader can find traces of Sozo lingering in this interview, as well as throughout Angela Carter's post-Japan writing. By now, it may be redundant for me to suggest how the relationship with Sozo Araki might have affected Carter's literary imagination. Something about Sozo or the relationship with him triggered her to write this much, and she seemed, as her postscripts show, to have returned repeatedly to her own journal writings, read them, and relive them again and again. They were an important source of inspiration for her literary imagination. I only hope this section and the memoir itself will provide the reader with more material for contemplation, and that they will contribute to a deeper exploration of the relation between Angela Carter's literature and her experiences in Japan, and to a further appreciation of her literary works, which are filled with nothing less than magical wonder.

---

[1] The research for this piece was made possible thanks to the support given by JSPS KAKENHI Grant Number JP24520307.

[2] The full argument on this work and Japan's influence on Carter's works can be found in my previously published article, 'Encounter with the Mirror of the Other: Angela Carter and Her Personal Connection with Japan,' in *Angelaki: Journal of the Theoretical Humanities*, vol.22, no.1, Mar. 2017, pp.77-92.

Works Consulted

Bell, Ronald, editor. *The Japan Experience*. Weatherhill, 1973.

Butler, Judith. 'Performative Acts and Gender Constitution: An Essay in Phenomenology and Feminist Theory.' *Theatre Journal*, vol. 44, no. 4, Dec. 1988, pp. 519-531.

Carter, Angela. *Angela Carter Papers*: *Japan 1*. British Library, London, Carter MS 88899/1/80.

---. *Angela Carter Papers: Journal*. British Library, London, Carter MS 88899/1/93.

---. *Angela Carter Papers: Journal*. British Library, London, Carter MS 88899/1/94.

---. *Burning Your Boats*. 1995. Vintage, 1996.

---. *Correspondence of Angela Carter and Carole Howells*, British Library, London, Carter MS 89102/1/93.

---. *Fireworks*. 1974. Virago, 1988.

---. *The Infernal Desire Machines of Doctor Hoffman*. 1972. Penguin, 1982.

---. *Nothing Sacred: Selected Writings*. Virago, 1982.

---. *Shaking a Leg: Collected Writings*. 1997. Penguin, 1998.

Gamble, Sarah. *Angela Carter: A Literary Life*. Palgrave Macmillan, 2006.

Gordon, Edmund. *The Invention of Angela Carter: A Biography*. Chatto & Windus, 2016.

Ikoma, Natsumi. 'Encounter with the Mirror of the Other: Angela Carter and Her Personal Connection with Japan.' *Angelaki: Journal of the Theoretical Humanities*, vol.22, no.1, Mar. 2017, pp. 77-92.

Sage, Lorna, editor. *Flesh and the Mirror: Essays on the Art of Angela Carter*. Virago, 1994.

Stevens, Wallace. *The Collected Poems*. 1954. Vintage, 1990.

Sozo Araki

He studied political science and economics at the Waseda University but dropped out before graduation. After studying in Canada, he started teaching English and working as a counselor. He has many publications in the area of popular psychology. Currently he lives in Tokyo with his wife.

Sozo Araki

Natsumi Ikoma

She received her Ph.D. from Durham University. Currently she is a professor of British and Japanese literature and gender studies at International Christian University in Japan. Her research interests cover the representation of the body in literature, gender performativity, and feminist theory. She writes extensively on the works of Angela Carter.

Seduced by Japan:
A Memoir of the Days Spent with Angela Carter
with "Her Side of the Story" written by Natsumi Ikoma

平成 29 年 11 月 20 日 印 刷	平成 29 年 11 月 30 日 発 行

著　　者 ⓒ 荒　木　創　造

訳　　者　　生　駒　夏　美

発　行　者　　佐　々　木　元

制作・発行所　株式会社 英　　宝　　社

〒 101-0032 東京都千代田区岩本町 2-7-7
☎ [03] (5833) 5870　Fax [03] (5833) 5872

ISBN 978-4-269-72147-0　C3098
[印刷・製本：モリモト印刷株式会社]